Too
CLOSE
to the
Flame

Too CLOSE to the *Flame*

Recognizing and Avoiding
Sexualized Relationships

GREGORY L. JANTZ, PH.D.

WITH ANN MCMURRAY

HOWARD
PUBLISHING CO.

Our purpose at Howard Publishing is to:

- *Increase faith* in the hearts of growing Christians
- *Inspire holiness* in the lives of believers
- *Instill hope* in the hearts of struggling people everywhere

Because He's coming again!

Published by Howard Publishing Co., Inc.,
3117 North 7th Street, West Monroe, Louisiana 71291-2227
03 04 05 06 07 08 09 10 11 12   10 9 8 7 6 5 4 3 2 1

Library of Congress Cataloging-in-Publication Data
Jantz, Gregory L.
     Too close to the flame : recognizing and avoiding sexualized relationships /
Gregory L. Jantz, with Ann McMurray.
          p. cm.
     ISBN 1-58229-332-5 (PBK)
     1. Sexual deviation. 2. Sexual deviation—Biblical teaching. 3. Conduct of life.
I. McMurray, Ann. II. Title.

HQ71.J36 1999
306.77—dc21
                                                                99-047272

Edited by Gene Shelburne
Interior design by Stephanie Denney
Cover design by LinDee Loveland

Scripture quotations not otherwise marked are taken from the Holy Bible, New International Version. Copyright ©1973, 1978, 1984 International Bible Society. Used by permission of Zondervan Bible Publishers. Other Scriptures are quoted from The Holy Bible, Authorized King James Version (KJV), ©1961 by The National Publishing Co.

Anecdotes in this volume are based on fact; however, in some instances details have been changed to protect identities.

Publisher's Note: Because everyone's particular situation is unique, the ideas and suggestions contained in this book should not be considered a substitute for consultation with a psychiatrist or trained therapist.

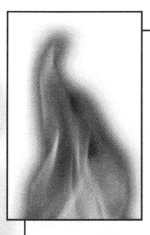

May the words in this book
heal and protect the precious
gift of our relationships.

CONTENTS

ACKNOWLEDGMENTS

This book was carefully crafted by the writing skills of my colleague, Ann McMurray. I am blessed by our partnership. I would also like to express my sincere thanks to Philis Boultinghouse and Gene Shelburne for the thoughtful help and invaluable insights they provided during the editing phase. Their biblical understanding and care for the text was a blessing.

INTRODUCTION

A Message for You

In a world filled with members of the opposite sex, your chances of coming into contact with them are pretty high. Men will be your fathers, brothers, coworkers, friends, and husbands. Women will be your mothers, sisters, coworkers, friends, and wives. This book is written to help you recognize and avoid potentially dangerous opposite-sex relationships.

Our only dependable basis for this discernment comes not from the culture, not from family traditions, and not from personal choices. Culture has a way of shifting its mores from era to era, swept along by the critical mass of current opinion. Family traditions have a way of perpetuating improper behavior, duplicating the sins of previous generations along with genetic material. Personal choices have a way of leading to unintended consequences, with feelings and desires ascendant and caution thrown to the wind.

In the midst of uncertainty like this, we have only one standard to go by—the one articulated by the creator of man and woman, by the author of male and female, by the originator of the very concept of sex, God himself. This book will use God's Word as the standard to accomplish several objectives. One is to help you recognize which sexual relationships are God-sanctioned and which are God-prohibited. Another goal is to give you the tools you need to recognize which relationships have a tendency toward sexualization and how to respond in case they do. This book will also help you recognize those individuals who may tend to sexualize relationships. You'll learn what to do if you encounter such a person. You'll also learn what to do if you are one.

The subject of our sexuality can be a controversial one. At times, the pages that follow will contain graphic descriptions vividly depicting the dilemmas posed by sexualized relationships. The reason for such explicitness is to ensure that sin be seen as sin and that it be stripped of any veil of secrecy or acceptability. Care has been used to be respectful of those who have been victims of inappropriately sexualized relationships; at the same time, this book will boldly confront those who sexualize relationships when they should not. This book arises from a knowledge of the severity of the problem and a sincere desire to provide hope and healing for all who read its pages.

Chapters 11 through 15 will deal specifically with situations that arise out of relationships between counselors or pastors and those they help. Spiritual and emotional advisors are particularly vulnerable to inappropriately sexualized relationships. During the past ten years, the front pages of newspapers and the lead stories on the evening news have heralded the infidelities of pastors and counselors for all to see.

If you are a counselor or pastor and have been in your profession for very long, you probably know at least one, perhaps more, of your colleagues who have engaged in inappropriate behavior with someone they were working with. You may even have succumbed to the temptation yourself.

"Strengthen your feeble arms and weak knees," the Scriptures admonish us. "Make level paths for your feet, so that the lame may not be disabled, but rather healed" (Hebrews 12:12–13). Our weakness can further cripple those who look to us for strength. We need to enhance our skills and hone our wisdom through studies like this one. If our failure causes someone else to fall, they are apt to take us down with them.

People and situations described in this book have been altered to protect privacy and identity. The stories are provided to illustrate our points, not to furnish specific details or clinical case studies.

"Watch and pray so that you will not fall into temptation," our Lord warned his men (Mark 14:38).

This book can help you to watch. It can increase your discernment, enhancing your relational eyesight so that you can see ahead of time the sexual risks that loom in your path.

By reading this book you are acknowledging the presence of One greater than yourself, who sees your relationships and desires for them to be pure and helpful to all concerned.

By reading this book you are acknowledging the reality that temptations will come and, if you're not careful, cause you to fall.

THE POWERFUL,
INVASIVE INFLUENCE
OF CURRENT CULTURE
SEEPS INTO OUR
CONSCIOUSNESS
MOMENT BY MOMENT,
AND WE HARDLY
KNOW IT.

1

Without wood a fire goes out.
—Proverbs 26:20

RECOGNIZE
THE KINDLING OF CURRENT CULTURE

The Tinderbox We Live in Today

O ur world is aflame with sex. Sex is practiced openly, talked about freely, engaged in creatively, and flaunted shamelessly. Cultural stigmas that once kept sex within definable boundaries have been debunked by the gurus of this age. Few people seem to know the rules for sexual behavior. Television networks flaunt homosexuality on prime time soaps like *The Practice*. Advertisers invade our living rooms with crudity and nudity that would have cost TV stations their broadcast licenses a few decades ago. As a result, the fire of sexuality burns in the souls of all of us at a dangerous temperature. Even those of us who have confessed Christ as Lord and who intend to share his holiness find that our hearts and minds have been saturated to an alarming degree by the incessant bombardment of sexual images and sexual language. Almost without knowing it happened, the present generation has become blasé about sexual humor and seductive shows that would have outraged our grandparents. We soak up Jay Leno's innuendos and Victoria's Secret's advertising porn with hardly a flicker of complaint or concern. And we who have been called by the Lord to be a holy people seem to be hardly conscious of the levels of lust kindled within us by our constant daily immersion in prurience. Our tolerance level for degrading sexual behavior and expression has risen year by year, searing our consciences and silencing inhibitions that should protect our hearts and minds. Our sexual desires are constantly being stoked by the culture we live in, and many of us are at risk because a dangerous fire smolders within.

It's in the Air We Breathe

In Denton, Texas, a group of cheerleaders find themselves in the midst of a controversy. For a year they have been performing a dance routine with a song called "Barbie Girl," and now, right before an important competition, some parents object. The coach is indignant. Having to learn new material at this late date will hurt their chances of winning. According to the Associated Press story, the coach is upset because "some freaked-out parents" complain that the song is "suggestive." Its lyrics include: "You can brush my hair, undress me everywhere / Kiss me here, touch me there, hanky-panky."

What do you think? Is this just a case of prudish parents interfering with the coach's choice of innocent dance material? Would it change your opinion if we told you that the cheerleaders are girls four to six years old?

If you missed that story in your newspaper, you know all about this one.

A beauty queen is murdered in Colorado. Speculation arises that sexual abuse occurred prior to her death by strangulation. Across the country her image stares out from the covers of magazines and supermarket tabloids. Big eyes with mascara-enhanced lashes, fluffed blonde hair, and perfectly painted red lips give urgency to the question everybody wants to know: How did she die? Stories detail her home life and display pictures taken at pageant competitions. Her glamorous hair, stylish outfits, and expertly applied cosmetics accentuate an already beautiful face.

The pictures, however, are eerie, and not just because they show the eyes of the dead. They disturb us because this beauty queen should have had more in common with Barney than with Barbie. She should have been more acquainted with grass-stained knees than with painted lips. She should have spent more time combing a doll's hair than having her own hair teased and curled. She should have spent more time learning how to ride a bike or climb a tree than learning how to walk down a pageant runway or how to smile with just the right amount of pout. Jon Benet Ramsey was just six years old when she was murdered.

Children often act as a mirror, starkly reflecting the values of the society they live in. In them we see transparent images made up of pudgy flesh, their wide eyes a window into the priorities decreed by society at large. Children become the backdrop upon which culture projects what it finds most desirable. Our oversexed culture produced those minicheerleaders singing about hanky-panky. It cost Jon Benet her childhood and probably her life. If they watch TV, second-graders today know more about homosexuality and bedroom activity than their grandparents did when they started college. In an age when we fast-forward our children into the realm of sexuality long before puberty sets in, can anybody doubt that our culture is obsessed with sex?

The sexualizing of our era is not something Christians can shrug their shoulders at, as if they lived on Mars instead of on this sex-maddened globe called Earth. None of us lives in a vacuum. If we live in an age that challenges integrity in personal relationships, we'd better look closely at our own relationships. If we live in a culture that continually blares sexual messages, it's not enough to subconsciously turn down the volume. We'd better do some serious soul-searching to see how many of those messages we have unknowingly absorbed. Knowing what the messages are and how they are transmitted is one of the first steps to closing our hearts and ears to the unholy impulses they would stir within us.

Our Culture Adds Fuel to the Sexual Fire

The powerful, invasive influence of current culture seeps into our consciousness moment by moment, and we hardly know it. Everything we see, everything we hear shapes our thoughts and drives our actions. From the time we wake up to the time we lie down, we are inundated by our culture's messages. We read them. We talk about them. We internalize them. Even if we don't actually think much about them.

As we ingest and assimilate the assumptions that underlie our culture, it is inevitable that our own values and resultant behavior will change. What was previously unacceptable becomes acceptable. What was questioned before, we now do without a second thought. In a culture that has abandoned most of its stigmas about sex outside of marriage, it would be a miracle if Christians did not find themselves winking at behavior they once knew to be unholy. How many of us who once knew better now allow ourselves to enjoy the dalliance of some person with whom we have no moral right to act, feel, or talk sexually? In a culture that has lowered its barriers, sex intrudes today into many inappropriate places, and all of us are increasingly at risk because of it.

Movies as Kindling

If you've been watching movies for the last half of the twentieth century, you know that Hollywood has drastically changed during that time. Gone are the dapper flair of Cary Grant, the pent-up intensity of Ingrid Bergman, the rugged masculinity of Humphrey Bogart, the silky sophistication of Grace Kelley. Gone are the impish innocence of Doris Day, the solid fidelity of Jimmy Stewart, the controlled passion of Deborah Kerr, the no-nonsense sensibility of Spencer Tracy. Gone also are intimacy implied with veiled looks, solitary embraces, and heated kisses that went no farther on the screen. Sex has come out from behind the door of the closed bed-

4

room. With each season of prime-time rating wars, the networks vie to see who can push the sexual envelope one notch farther, who can graphically display more skin, who can introduce America's families to the most shocking forms of sexual perversion, and Hollywood trolls for Oscars by abandoning all shame.

"Adults only" used to imply that a film featured a sexual relationship between unmarried partners. Today it has become a badge of honor used to attract those who desire explicitly pornographic filth. PG-13 films expose viewers to thinly disguised sexual encounters, usually between unmarried teens or young adults. Since these encounters are portrayed as romantic and inevitable, often taking place as the culmination of the movie's plot, they are eagerly anticipated by those who have paid to watch them—including the adolescents in the audience. Thus, in the venue our culture calls entertainment, we deliver the repeated, cleverly packaged message that sex is the natural consequence of true love and that it should be unencumbered by the realities of life. The sad truth is that for many men and women today these scenes of misplaced sexual activity *are* real life. But Hollywood always seems to forget to tell us about the tragic consequences of such behavior.

Through the schoolhouse of the theater, Americans are being led to believe that nothing must hamper the sexual culmination of a true-love relationship—not age, not the absence of a marriage license, not the fact that you are married to somebody else. The main characters in a movie may not survive to its end, but everything is somehow all right if they at least had sex before they drew their last breath.

Television as Kindling

The line between TV and movies has blurred with the advent of VCRs and DVDs. Films made for TV and films made for the silver screen vary little in content, but the television films may wield by far the greater influence on our thinking and behavior. They invade our homes night after night. Once the television set was a techno-logical marvel around which the traditional family huddled while they watched variety shows or comedy hours in the early evening. Today television has become the white noise of our age, always on in the background of our lives. We eat dinner by it, do homework by it, do housework while it drones on, and even pretend to social-ize in spite of its distractions.

Anybody who has watched the daytime soaps knows that pro-ducers hype their ratings by loading their shows with the sexually explicit or unusual. It's hard for even the most dedicated soap fan to keep up with who's in bed with whom from week to week, and the bed-hopping is enacted with increasingly graphic performances. Little is left to the imagination. Daytime talk shows routinely troll the cultural waters for the sexually deviant, snagging any bizarre relationship and showing off aberrant catches as trophies during the ratings sweeps. Meanwhile the sitcoms at night treat viewers to humor that would disgrace fourth-grade boys behind an outhouse.

Worse than the shows on TV are the accumulated hours of sex-oriented advertising. Capturing households is no longer enough to sell high-dollar advertising time to corporate sponsors. The age of the typical viewer of the spots often matters more than the number of viewers, because the viewers' age bracket equates to disposable income. Did you know that TV advertisers have identified eighteen-to-thirty-four-year-olds as the big spenders? To lure these viewers, networks in the past few years have opted for shows that reflect this age-group's open sexual attitudes and their obsession with sexual themes. So good-bye to *Murder She Wrote* and *Dr. Quinn, Medicine Woman* and hello to *Living Single* and *Friends*.

Cable and satellite TV allow some worthwhile programming to find a syndicate home, but these relatively new technologies also allow vast new levels of pornography to flood into our homes. Independent networks, once the last bastion of decent family pro-gramming, increasingly seem to be choosing to cater to a prurient clientele by producing and showing sexier material. Pay-per-view pornography is as close as the cable box in millions of homes.

Magazines as Kindling

We don't want to belabor the point that we live in a culture saturated with sex, but we do want to alert you to some sources that may be affecting the lives and hearts of some unsuspecting Christians. It's vital that we identify sources of sexualization in our culture in order to reduce the exposure for our own souls.

Ever since the glory days of *Playboy*, men's magazines have been devoted to showcasing women as sex objects, the value of the articles aside. Few people ever bought the line that *Playboy* was a forum for serious philosophy or current events, did they? But the Hugh Hefner stuff from the sexy sixties appears tame when compared to the newer variations of the genre. No picture is too revealing. No position too lurid. No pairing too pornographic. These magazines are dedicated to the sexual arousal of their readers. To keep producing this effect, the publishers have to supply increasingly graphic images. Prurience is a hungry beast that craves an ever-larger and dirtier diet to satiate its appetite. Defenders of this sort of journalism insist that these journals provide only pleasure without harm. Some even tout this kind of pornography as a way to reduce sexual crimes, although hard statistics from law-enforcement agencies always verify the opposite effect. By fostering the image of women within a tightly confined sexual lens, they have been one of the strongest factors in accelerating the sexualization of our society.

While women's magazines usually do not contain the same level of sexual imagery as the men's publications, still they contribute deleteriously to our sexually charged culture. They influence the social climate through the presentation of ideas rather than graphics. Some of these magazines target adolescent females. Others aim at more mature women. But their message is always the same: Men are to be viewed as sexual quarry. They offer tips for capturing and keeping alive a sexual relationship, offering detailed instructions on how to talk and act to entrap the intended lover and how to respond sexually to keep the man once they ensnare him. According to a study done in late 1996 by public relations firm DeChant-Hughes of Chicago, almost three-quarters of the articles published in women's magazines today are devoted to sexual topics. Have you paid any attention lately to the magazines available in the checkout line at your nearby supermarket? Even a cursory perusal will confirm the sexual content. Helpful sidebars fill you in on what a desirable man "wants in a woman." Typical articles portray the establishment of male-female relationships as a grand strategy with sex as the end prize.

Targeting preadolescent girls as young as ten or eleven, many of these magazines have adopted a sexuality-as-strategy concept. According to the study cited above, sexual topics make up 63 percent of the articles in the magazines for teenage females. Instead of advising girls to postpone sexual activity until they are married, these magazines advocate safe sex. Their "wise" counsel is "Wait until you are ready for a 'committed' relationship," and "Always use contraceptives to avoid unplanned pregnancies and sexually transmitted diseases. But, by all means, enjoy sex!"

Do you suppose our kids are confused? We tell them "Just Say No" to drugs, but use a condom when having sex. Our culture for the most part has conceded the battle for chastity. A recent poll for *U.S. News & World Report* found that 74 percent of the Americans asked had serious qualms about teens having sex before marriage. But federally financed TV ads and sex-education programs give millions of girls the opposite message. Condoms are in, they preach. Abstinence is unrealistic.

Thanks to our ever-younger conditioning, preadolescent girls have much more time to worry about their weight, to learn how to apply exactly the right shade of eye shadow, to agonize over which makeup is right for their skin type, and to worry about which outfit is more likely to catch the attention of that special guy. In other words, they get to spend their childhood trying to look, talk, dress, and act like adults. The time bomb is ticking long before they are old enough to understand the consequences of their budding sexuality.

Music as Kindling

Have you paid attention lately to the lyrics of the songs broadcast by your local radio stations? Gone are most of the euphemisms songwriters used in past years to comply with FCC restrictions. Today sex is sung about and rapped about without any masking or shading. Violent sexual themes are highlighted to market certain musical groups or recordings. Listen to the "top ten" country and western or rock songs, and you'll find it hard to believe that radio stations are governed by any limits of decency or propriety. Tolerance and insensitivity are equated with sophistication. As if to say, "What's the big deal? I've heard and seen worse."

Advertising as Kindling

Sex sells. Plaster half-naked poster girls in seductive poses across a full-page ad for Breakfast Barley Flakes and the sales of the cereal evidently will go up. Personal care products, ranging from shaving cream to dandruff shampoo, promise us that their brand will give us an edge in opposite-sex attraction. Certain brands of clothing are routinely touted as the quickest route to being unclothed. Both the scent names and the packaging of some popular fragrances simulate mating.

Sex therapist Dr. Gerald Rogers did an informal six-month study of print-media ads that used sex as their hook. The result was a lengthy presentation of rapidly viewed slides of hundreds of sexy advertisements. Whenever he showed the series to a gathering of his colleagues in the medical and counseling fields, their response was invariably one of shock and dismay. Especially when Dr. Rogers revealed to them that the array of titillating ads came from everyday newspapers and "family" magazines that most of them had on their coffee tables.

Avant-garde, obscure forms of sexual innuendo lace today's advertisements, with the menu of sexual images growing more blatant both in print and over the airwaves with each passing season. Sheets askew, intertwined legs, and slivers of uncovered flesh no longer seem to shock the average viewer of page or screen. Have you heard the TV spots that use the auditory equivalent of a woman reaching orgasm to suggest that a certain product is satisfying? It suggests also that our society is rapidly losing any sense of shame.

CURRENT CULTURE ERASES SEXUAL BOUNDARIES

In the decades since the sexual revolution of the sixties, our culture has drastically shifted its system of sexual values. What used to be considered decent and proper society now lampoons as anachronistic or discards as oppressive. Boundaries that in the past acted as a buffer for sexual behavior have been demolished, opening the gates for freer access to overtly sexual expression. Consider some of the changes in recent times.

Virginity Devalued / Sexual Equality Elevated

According to the Centers for Disease Control and Prevention, almost half of today's ninth-graders say they have already had sexual intercourse. This means that by the time our kids reach the ripe old age of fourteen, over half of them say they've already lost their virginity.

Children are like the rest of us. They have values. They value their independence and put up a constant struggle to assert their ideas of freedom. They value their friendships, often choosing the influence of friends over that of parents. They value their leisure activities. Guess what most of them will choose if you offer them a choice between playing video games or going online versus doing homework or spending time in family events. If you've raised a teenager or two, you know how fiercely adolescents will fight to maintain their "rights" and values. But according to the CDC report we cited, half of the ninth-graders in America did not value their virginity enough to keep it.

Should it surprise us that today's children mirror the attitudes of today's adults toward virginity? Virginity is an endangered species in the modern adult world. Young adults are waiting longer to marry. As divorce rates have risen, the number of unattached adults among us has risen. And the very idea that all these unmarried adults should remain sexually inactive often is hooted at both by media muckrakers and by serious educational experts. In the *U.S. News* poll mentioned earlier, fewer than half of the respondents under forty-five thought it was a good idea to remain a virgin until marriage. The majority of those polled felt that having premarital sexual partners makes it easier for a person to pick out a compatible spouse. In fact, premarital sex was characterized as "beneficial" by a majority of the sub-forty-five group. In their eyes, premarital sex is beneficial, virginity is not.

Sexual equality is another plank in the argument for unrestricted sexual activity. The rationale purports that today's sexual freedom corrects oppressive restrictions of the past. Women were shortchanged in sexual relationships because of the possibility of pregnancy, we are told. But today, with birth control methods and abortion easily available, requiring female virginity is archaic. Consequence-free sex is now the right of women, just as it has been for men, the argument claims. Unrestricted sexual activity is touted as one way for a woman to declare her gender freedom.

Fidelity Devalued / Personal Fulfillment Elevated

Gerald was devastated. Maggie had just told him she didn't love him anymore. Without a tear in her eye she explained that after twenty-six years she didn't want to be married to him any longer. No, she said, there wasn't anyone else. Gerald almost wished there had been. He could have understood that better. Maggie said she just didn't feel the same way about him as she used to. She couldn't remember when her feelings changed. There just hadn't been anything there for a while. She'd finally grown tired of pretending all the time. Now she just wanted out. She didn't hate him, she said. She just didn't love him. She figured she had a little less than half her life left, and she wanted to start doing things for herself, taking care of herself, for a change. There wasn't anybody else, but Gerald got the feeling she wouldn't mind if there were.

Maggie left Gerald with a gaping hole in his life. He was getting older. So were his knees and joints, worn out by hard labor on construction jobs. He had been looking forward to slowing down, spending some good years with Maggie now that the kids were grown. And all this time she had been looking forward to spending her good years without him. They'd grown apart, Maggie told him. They didn't want the same things in life anymore. She wouldn't explain exactly what those things were, just that they were different from what he wanted. Gerald could not understand that. He had dreamed of growing old with her, and his dream had become her nightmare.

He tried to talk her out of it, apologizing for working too hard, for spending too many evenings after work at the bar, for not going to enough school functions when the kids were small, for not saying "I love you" enough. He told her he'd make it up to her if she'd just stay and give him another chance. She actually stopped a moment and thought about it. Thought about it and still said no.

Just as virginity has been devalued by the world we live in, so has exclusivity and longevity in sexual relationships. Feelings, not fidelity, have been elevated within relationships by our culture. If you are unhappy in your present relationship, conventional wisdom tells you that you're duty-bound to leave. The only thing that binds you to your spouse is how well your needs are being met within the marriage. Examples of couples calling it quits even after years of marriage, abound both around the corner and in the national spot-light. Seeing it happen so often fuels "the middle-age crazies" in some of us and plants the seed of temptation for unsatisfied spouses to explore greener pastures.

Today counselors and pastors observe the phenomenon of people whose lifelong pattern is one of investigating life outside their current relationships. They go from relationship to relation-ship, forming and breaking liaisons simply on the basis of how they *feel* at any given moment. Personal fulfillment is their god. Their right. They deserve to be in a happy relationship. So they keep searching until they find the "right" person. Such behavior has con-sequences for all of us. As it becomes more fashionable to drop out of relationships, the pool of sexually active potential partners grows ever larger, and the threat to existing marriages escalates.

Moral Absolutes Devalued / Situational Ethics Elevated

Outside our church walls where Bible-believing people still teach and believe that God's moral laws are immutable standards for human behavior lies a radically different culture that denies the very existence of truth. According to this view of life, no person has the right to tell any other person that their ideas or their behavior are wrong. Right and wrong are simply what each person thinks they are, depending on their particular circumstance. Sometimes this the-ory has been called situation ethics, meaning that ethical standards are determined by individual situations, not by any set of unchang-ing standards.

We can no longer say, "Thou shalt not commit adultery." What if you're trapped in a loveless marriage with a distant, unaffectionate spouse, and by chance you happen to meet an attractive, vibrant, compassionate soul mate with whom you make an immediate, consuming connection? Who could be hardhearted enough to expect you to remain trapped in a dead-end relationship when ulti-mate happiness awaits you in the arms of your newfound truelove?

The "situation" demands that old-fashioned fetters such as marriage vows and family responsibilities take a backseat to our immediate opportunity for gratification. You may not have spent much time agonizing over the intricacies of modern ethical theories, but chances are high that the scenario we've just described has been played out time and again among your kinfolks, neighbors, and associates. And you've seen the wreckage of lives left in the wake of people who proclaimed that "it must be good because it feels so right."

The God who made us and who desires our well-being and happiness made rules to keep us from getting hurt. His rules for living have been replaced in our culture by a single rule. This rule says that no rules exist except the one that says you must tolerate all opinions and lifestyles as being equally valid. Divine rules that once sanctified and preserved our core relationships have been jettisoned by a culture that makes personal fulfillment its ultimate goal. We live in a world full of Geralds and Maggies, whose pitiful quests for happiness outside the Creator's boundaries have cost them the stability of relationship and the dependability of love on which true happiness must rest. Our culture applauds Maggie's pluck, while it carefully ignores the tears and turmoil caused by her decision to forget sacred promises.

CULTURAL SHIFTS CONTRIBUTE TO SEXUAL CONFUSION

Life is certainly a lot more complicated than it used to be. One reason for this is the confusion and misunderstandings caused by rapid shifts in male-female roles.

Gentlemen have been expected to open doors for ladies for at least two centuries. Sometimes they still do. A man who opens the door for a woman loaded down with packages is still considered polite. But if a fellow opens the door for a woman without encumbrances today, she may think he's condescending. After all, does he think she's too dense to fathom the door mechanism or too lacking in muscles to open it for herself? How does a guy know what to do?

It's just as hard for the ladies. A woman who argues vehemently for a specific point of view in a meeting with a large group is considered professionally aggressive. But a woman who argues just as aggressively for a specific point of view one-on-one may be considered shrewish or needlessly confrontational.

Heightened sensitivities to sexual harassment can make things really sticky. A woman who engages in sexually charged conversation around the lunch table at work tends to be accepted as a person who's trying to be a part of the group. But a male colleague who participates in her sexually loaded conversation can easily get himself fired as a sexual harasser.

To this confusion of roles add the ever-shifting behavior rules of situation ethics and you've got a recipe for bewilderment and chaos. Men and women today are never quite sure where they're supposed to stand. If they get it figured out, by tomorrow the rules of the game are almost certain to have changed.

Wife, Mother, and Male-Protector Roles

The number of Americans who were alive before World War II is dwindling. If you were born since then, can you imagine a world where nice women worked only as teachers, nurses, secretaries, or waitresses? These were "women's professions," and the minority of women who filled them worked almost exclusively with other women. Before the Great War, no females were soldiers, firefighters, production managers, carpenters, or corporate CEOs. Women who did work outside the home still derived their primary sense of identity as somebody's wife or mother or—if they were unmarried—somebody's daughter, and men everywhere related to women on the basis of these domestic roles. Society dictated that you did not chase another man's wife, you did not act disreputably toward another man's daughter, and you always showed respect to someone

15

else's mother. In that pre-war world a man was no gentleman if he behaved toward a woman in a way that was considered inappropriate and unseemly. Women merited special courtesy and protection. "Women and children first," they cried when the *Titanic* deployed her lifeboats. What do you suppose they would shout today? Somehow, during the final decades of the twentieth century, the special honor and respect traditionally apportioned to women both by social custom and by law came to be perceived as a patronizing put-down—often because the obvious difference in the roles of women and men made some men fancy that they were stronger and smarter and better than the objects of their courtesy and protection.

Rosie the Riveter

As American industry geared up to supply our armed forces during World War II, the social floodgates opened. Women found themselves called upon to assume traditional male trades in order to sustain the war effort. With millions of our men fighting on the beaches of Normandy and slogging through the jungles of Iwo Jima, someone had to run the factories, and women were elected. Although many women gladly exchanged their wrenches and grease guns for diapers and laundry soap after our soldiers came home, things never were the same. Once firmly ensconced in the marketplace, women have continued to enter and excel in areas of employment previously closed to them. The twofold effects were:

1. When large numbers of women left home to work, the long-standing practice of viewing a woman within her family context got hazed over. Women now began to stand on their own apart from their family ties. No longer were they just another man's wife or daughter or mother. They were now seen as independent people in their own right, capable of their own decisions without male permission or approval.

2. For the first time in our culture it became okay for decent women to be viewed openly as objects of sexual interest.

Can you see how the second effect compounded the first? As women began to be legitimate objects of sexual interest—both to men and to themselves—there was a marked increase in the areas and frequency of women's personal interactions with men outside their families. The result was predictable. Combine women, flush with the realization of their new power as independent persons, with men who can now view them as objects of sexual desire, and you can only expect sexual interactions to explode. Society would never be the same. For half a century now we have been struggling to find sensible guidelines that can give us some degree of safety and comfort in a sex-conscious world where men and women work and play together every day.

Loading Up the Moving Van

One contributing factor we can't overlook is the increasingly mobile nature of our society where men and women may switch careers and coasts every few years. Behavior patterns inevitably change when people are uprooted from their relational contexts. In other words, if Mary and Tom stay in Everytown, Minnesota, their neighbors will know Mary primarily as Tom's wife (and maybe even as John's daughter). And they know Tom as Mary's husband. The longer Mary and Tom live in Everytown, the more they and their neighbors interact within the context of their relationship as husband and wife. Phil may want to consider a sexual relationship with Mary, but their kids are on the same Little League team, and Phil bowls with Tom every other Thursday night, so he backs off.

If Tom and Mary move across the country, however, Ben might meet Mary at work. He's never met Mary's husband and never seen her kids. All he knows is Mary, outside her other relationships, so it's much easier for Ben to consider Mary as a suitable object of sexual pursuit than it was for Phil back in Everytown.

Mobility removes people from structured, ethical situations. Once our turf changes, the possibility for change in other areas becomes easier to contemplate. When you're a long way from home, things that once were tied down have a way of coming loose.

This Is the Army, Ms. Jones

Not everybody in our land has been happy about the inclusion of women in what used to be male jobs. One of the first groups to protest were the wives of the firefighters and police who already had those jobs. Understandably, they didn't want their husbands thrown together with other women in intense jobs where coworkers have to operate in close proximity, eating, bunking, and killing idle hours together. The likelihood of illicit sexual interaction in such circumstances should be obvious to anybody past puberty.

Nowhere has this objection proved more prescient than in the integration of women into the armed forces. Touched off by the Tailhook flap, scandals involving sexual interaction between members of the military, both consensual and forced, have been headline news for at least a decade. Within the span of one year, the U.S. Army was rocked with sexual assault charges leveled at a variety of male drill instructors, who were accused by female recruits of pressuring them for sexual favors. In addition, Master Sergeant of the Army, Gene McKinney, was accused by a number of former coworkers and aides of sexually propositioning them. Even within the rigid structures of the services, the proximity of men and women working side by side has led to sexualized relationships. Healthy young men and women confined in the bowels of a battleship or an aircraft carrier for months on end will likely find something more exciting than pinochle to pass their time. The number of pregnancies begun at sea is one stat the navy would just as soon we didn't know.

─────── Fuel for Thought ───────

Each chapter in this book will end with a "Fuel for Thought" section. This section will give you an opportunity to evaluate and apply what you've learned throughout the chapter. In order to get the maximum benefit from these questions, you might consider recording your answers (and enough of the question to jog your memory) in a spiral notebook or binder. Taking the time to think about and write down your responses will help you think through these issues in a more personal and helpful way.

This first chapter has been a long one with a lot to think about. Culture affects us from so many different angles. It is worth the effort, however, to begin to identify how your own attitudes and values have been (and are being) molded by society. Save this final section of the chapter for a quiet moment when you can work through the following questions. Taking sufficient time to answer honestly will allow you to gain useful insights about yourself. If an answer or thought is painful or unpleasant, don't shy away from it. Honestly contemplate the implications of your answers.

1. Write down the names of movies you have seen, either in a theater or on video, over the past six months. What was each of them rated? Were there sexual situations in each movie? What were the sexual messages given by each film?

2. Which television shows do you make it a point to see on a regular basis, if any? Beside their names, estimate the percentage of time each gives for plot or content that is sexual in nature.

3. Make a list of the magazines you subscribe to. If you are a man, would you keep each of them on your coffee table for public viewing? If you are a woman, has the sexual content of any publication you subscribe to ever caused you to write a letter to the editor or refuse to read an article?

4. What is your favorite radio station? Which style of music do you prefer? Have you ever been embarrassed because of the sexual content of the lyrics in a song you were listening to?

Would you turn off the radio or change stations if your grandmother walked in?

5. As you watch television or read print ads, do you enjoy seeing someone of the opposite sex in a suggestive pose? If an ad is sexy, do you find yourself taking more interest in the product being sold? Do you often give such an ad a second look?

6. Think back to your upbringing. In your family, how were women treated? How were men treated? Was one gender given preferential treatment over the other? In what ways?

7. In your current job do you work side-by-side with someone of the opposite sex? Have you ever thought about someone at work in a sexual way?

8. Are you a person who enjoys the attention of members of the opposite sex? If so, why do you enjoy being noticed by them? Do you draw attention to yourself if you feel you aren't being noticed?

Helpful Resource: The changing sexual landscape can be devastating to men. Adrift and rudderless on an uncharted sea, men can sail in circles, feeling overwhelmed and unsure of what to say to women or how to act around them. Since men generally are not given to revealing their personal feelings, they choose to deal with these challenges alone. Patrick A. Means has written a helpful book called *Men's Secret Wars.* Published by Revell, this fine work reveals the secret struggles of men in today's society and provides insight and help winning those battles.

MAY GOD GRANT YOU CLARITY *of mind as you come to recognize the effect culture has in your life. May he grant you strength of heart to honestly confront past patterns of thought.*

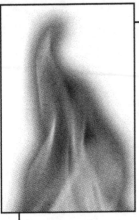

IN THE SPRING, AT THE TIME WHEN KINGS GO OFF TO WAR, David sent Joab out with the king's men. But David remained in Jerusalem.

One evening David walked around on the roof of the palace. From the roof he saw a woman bathing. The woman was very beautiful, and David sent someone to find out about her. The man said, "Isn't this Bathsheba, the wife of Uriah the Hittite?" Then David sent messengers to get her. She came to him, and he slept with her. Then she went back home. The woman conceived and sent word to David, saying, "I am pregnant."

So David sent this word to Joab: "Send me Uriah the Hittite." And Joab sent him to David. David said to Uriah, "Go down to your house and wash your feet." Uriah left the palace but slept at the entrance to the palace with his master's servants and did not go to his house.

Uriah said to David, "The ark and Israel and Judah are staying in tents, and my master Joab and my lord's men are camped in the open fields. How could I go to my house to eat and drink and lie with my wife?"

David said to him, "Stay here one more day, and tomorrow I will send you back." At David's invitation, he ate and drank with him, and David made him drunk. But in the evening Uriah went out to sleep among his master's servants; he did not go home.

In the morning David wrote a letter to Joab and sent it with Uriah. In it he wrote, "Put Uriah in the front line where the fighting is fiercest. Then withdraw from him so he will be struck down and die."

So while Joab had the city under siege, he put Uriah at a place where he knew the strongest defenders were. When the men of the city came out and fought against Joab, some of the men in David's army fell; moreover, Uriah the Hittite died.

Joab sent David a full account of the battle. He instructed the messenger: "When you have finished giving the king this account of the battle, the king's anger may flare up, and he may ask you, 'Why did you get so close to the city to fight?' If he asks you this, then say to him, 'Also, your servant Uriah the Hittite is dead.'"

When Uriah's wife heard that her husband was dead, she mourned for him. After the time of mourning was over, David had her brought to his house, and she became his wife and bore him a son. But the thing David had done displeased the Lord.

—from 2 Samuel 11

2

All a man's ways seem innocent to him, but motives are weighed by the LORD.
—Proverbs 16:2

AVOID
CULTURAL CONFUSION

Rely on the Rock,
Not on Shifting Sand

He stopped breathing altogether, heart hammering in his chest. She was just so gorgeous. In all the time they'd been dating, she'd never looked so good. She glided down the stairs to the entryway, smiling at him. Okay, he wasn't half-bad himself, in black tuxedo and combed back hair. Swallowing, he took her hands in his and choked out how wonderful she looked. Her cheeks flushed underneath the rouge. He could understand. He could feel it getting a little warm himself.

Her dress was full length to the floor, tapered at the waist, and cut low in the front. Piled up on the top of her head, a few errant curls of hair trickled down, resting along the curve of her neck. More than anything, he wanted to reach out and trace the line of curl down to the curve of warm skin. At that point her father cleared his throat and suggested they go into the living room for a picture of the happy couple. Slightly relieved, he hurriedly brushed a sudden drop of moisture from his upper lip.

Before long the pictures were done and they were out the door to his car. It seemed so inadequate for the evening. At least he'd taken the trouble to clean out the McDonald's cups and to take the gym bag out of the front seat. Gallantly he opened the passenger door for her and watched as she scooped up her skirt in her arms and ducked down to avoid hitting her hair on the top of the doorframe. Closing the door, he crossed over behind the car and got into the driver's side. Looking back at the house, he could see the living room curtains swish back into place.

Grinning broadly, he started the car and started their evening. Yes, it was their evening, the night of the Senior Prom. He knew how to get to the dance and where they were going for dinner. He just wasn't as sure where they were going from there. He knew how the evening was starting; he just wasn't as sure how it would end.

They chattered excitedly as he drove. In the back of his mind, though, a tension was growing. Unlike several other couples at school, they'd never had sex. Oh, they'd kissed and done a lot of touching, but had never actually had sex. After the summer was over, there'd be different colleges. Probably different lives. Tonight was when they were together. So the question loomed, should tonight be the night they really got together?

He knew what he'd heard, what he'd been told, what he'd been taught. And he certainly knew what he felt, or did he? When she'd walked down those stairs, thoughts had kind of taken a backseat to feelings. Now, looking over at her and the way her dress accentuated the curve of her breasts, it was all he could do to keep his thoughts out of the backseat.

He had a decision to make. She had a decision to make. It was a simple decision. So how come he was so confused?

In the first chapter we looked at the effect of culture and changing values on relationships today. So many factors come to bear, muddling a clear view of what is and is not acceptable sexual behavior. The range for misunderstanding and misstep is vast. With the sexual landscape in constant upheaval, what is the clear path to correct relationships?

With cultural messages bombarding us with sexual content, with sexual boundaries shifting and changing, what can we rely on to keep ourselves sexually steady? What can we use to anchor our relationships within their proper context?

Culture wants to decide for us. Media wants to decide for us. Friends want to decide for us. Everyone wants to decide for us. Go along with the popular trends, and we validate culture by adjusting ourselves to fit its form. Watch what they produce and buy what they sell, and we validate the media by acting according to demographic projection. Go along with the plans and values of others, and we validate friends by submerging our will into the group conscience. Go against the grain, and we are "countercultural." Strike out on our own, and media views us as "marginalized." Stand up to our friends, and we become outsiders. Yet this is precisely what God asks of us. "Do not conform...to the pattern of this world," he commands (Romans 12:2).

Standing alone in a crowd is painfully conspicuous. Being on your own can be very lonely. It's not fun to feel like you are the only person not chosen to play on the team, not culture's team or the media's team or the team that's got all of your friends. But standing on our own doesn't necessarily mean being on our own. If we choose wisely, we can position ourselves on the ultimate winning team.

AVOID GOING S-P-L-A-T

In Sunday school classrooms from California to Maine, anxious little faces gaze up at their teacher and watch intently as she sings. They watch her mouth move, see her hands out in front of her, and hear a simple little song fill the air: "The wise man built his house upon the Rock; the wise man built his house upon the Rock..."

Those of us who have spent any time in Bible class, or around children, probably know this song. It chronicles the parable Jesus tells in Luke 6:46–49:

> Why do you call me, "Lord, Lord," and do not do what I say? I will show you what he is like who comes to me and hears my words and puts them into practice. He is like a man building a house, who dug down deep and laid the foundation on rock. When a flood came, the torrent struck that house but could not shake it, because it was well built. But the one who hears my words and does not put them into practice is like a man who built a house on the ground without a foundation. The moment the torrent struck that house, it collapsed and its destruction was complete.

According to the words of the children's song, the wise man's house "stood firm," and the foolish man's house went "splat!" Somehow, in the years between childhood and adulthood, we forgot the simple concept of that song. God's Word is the foundation we are to use to avoid going "splat!" in our lives and in our relationships with members of the opposite sex.

God is the author of sex and sexuality. As the author, it only makes sense that he is the authority we are to go to when confronted with the question of how to carry on sexual relationships, no matter the time, no matter the situation. Just as the words of the song are simple, so is God's answer to sexualized relationships. God allows only one relationship to become sexualized. It is commonly known as marriage. Put even more simply, you are allowed to view only one person in a sexual way. God says you can have sex with only one person and still be pleasing to him. That one person is your husband or your wife.

If you are married, it's pretty simple whom you can enjoy a sexualized relationship with. If you are not married, and therefore have no spouse, it's even more simple. If you are not married, the Bible says you cannot have sex. If you are single, God allows no relationship in your life to be sexualized.

Only man, in his sin, could take such plain concepts and simple answers and turn sex today into such a complicated mess!

For This One Reason

In Genesis 2, God tells the beautiful story of the creation of woman to complete man. In verse 24, God says, "For this reason a man will leave his father and mother and be united to his wife, and they will become one flesh." Nowhere else in Scripture does God condone another kind of sexual relationship.

On the contrary, Scripture is full of admonitions to keep oneself sexually pure and apart from other sexual relationships. The Book of Proverbs contains numerous warnings to avoid sexual relations apart from marriage. Chapter 5, the last part of chapter 6, and all of chapter 7 are devoted to warnings against adultery.

Current culture paints a romantic picture of sex without regard to whom that sex is with. In fact, spouses often are portrayed as uninteresting and cold, while sex outside marriage is glamorized as exciting, real, and powerful. Listen to what God says in Proverbs 6:26: "The prostitute reduces you to a loaf of bread, and the adulteress preys upon your very life." Not very romantic, is it? God does not view life from a skewed perspective, camouflaging sinful activity in the rosy haze of romance. He sees life truthfully, clearly. He knows what the consequences are, for he not only sees the future—he *is* the future.

Current influences may tell you there are valid reasons for initiating and sustaining a sexual relationship outside of marriage. Read on in Proverbs 6 and listen to God's word in verses 27 through 29: "Can a man scoop fire into his lap without his clothes being burned? Can a man walk on hot coals without his feet being scorched? So is he who sleeps with another man's wife; no one who touches her will go unpunished."

Simple answers from God's Word lead to plain conclusions. If you are having sex with anyone other than your spouse, God does not approve. The culture may approve, the media may applaud, your friends may even admire you, but God says you will not go unpunished.

"May Your Fountain Be Blessed"

Do not be deceived. Culture whispers that God is mean and harsh. Culture reads the words above and says, "That's all God wants to do—punish you! He doesn't want you to enjoy life or have any fun! And he certainly doesn't want you to have a good time with sex!" With all of the admonitions in Scripture about the dangers of impurity and sex outside of marriage, a very real component of the "fear of God" is validated where sex is concerned.

Remember again, however, that God is the author of sex and marriage. It is not a fluke that men and women are attracted to each other. It is not by accident that sexual intercourse is pleasurable. It is no fluke or accident; it is God-designed. Culture may think it composed the symphony of sexual pleasure, but God invented the notes. Proverbs 5:18-19 gives this blessing from the Lord: "May your fountain be blessed, and may you rejoice in the wife of your youth. A loving doe, a graceful deer—may her breasts satisfy you always, may you ever be captivated by her love." God knows men and women will be attracted to each other and will enjoy sexual relations together. Sexual pleasure is not a result of a "sexually liberated" culture; it is the gift of God, offered within the marriage relationship.

In contrast to the sinner's being burned or scorched by engaging in unauthorized sex, God provides another image for marriage, one of a fountain with springs of cool water. God expects you to use your water wisely. Observe the imagery in Proverbs 5:15-18. It is very clear. "Drink water from your own cistern, running water from your own well. Should your springs overflow in the streets, your streams of water in the public squares? Let them be yours alone, never to be shared with strangers. May your fountain be blessed, and may you rejoice in the wife of your youth."

God has no problem with sex as he designed it, fully enjoyed and experienced by a husband and wife. It is within this God-designed environment that sexual activity can reach its promise and complete fulfillment. God—not culture—is the provider of true, romantic love.

The Eye-Heart Connection

God allows only one sexualized relationship: marriage. He does not expect men and women to completely segregate from each other so as not to sin, however. In the course of daily life, men and women will, and do, interact in relationships that are not sexual. God recognizes that male-female relationships can exist apart from sexual feelings and actions. God also recognizes that nonsexual male-female relationships can become sexualized if you are not careful to guard your eye.

Your eye? Not your actions? Not your heart?

Matthew 5:27–28 warns, "You have heard that it was said, 'Do not commit adultery.' But I tell you that anyone who looks at a woman lustfully has already committed adultery with her in his heart." It's not just what we see, it's the way we see it that leads us into sexual sin. Looking at a person of the opposite sex is not sinful. Looking at them as a target for illicit sexual gratification can plunge us quickly into sin. "The lust of the eyes," the Bible calls it (1 John 2:16 KJV). Our wandering eyes can get us into trouble.

In dealing with our sex-laden culture, we need to rely on God's Word to provide the framework necessary to construct a set of core beliefs that will maintain the view of the "impossibility" of certain sexualized behaviors and relationships. A heart committed to God's holiness can effectively censor a roving eye.

REPLACING BREACHED SOCIAL BARRIERS WITH CORE BELIEFS

The music was great. Everybody was there. He could see how her appearance affected the others at the dance. Some of the girls gushed about how gorgeous she was. Others looked critically, evaluating the results of her labor as compared to theirs. The guys stared appreciatively at her and enviously at him. Their unspoken challenge seemed to be, "So, what are you going to do about it?"

His own folks hadn't been much help, not that he'd ever go to them for advice about something like this, in the first place. The extent of his sex talk growing up was a regrettable episode when he was fourteen. His dad had taken him aside and told him he'd kill him if he ever knocked up a girl. Then, without another word, he'd handed over a small square package. There was no way he was going to tell his dad he already knew about condoms. They'd been told all about them in school. He hadn't thrown it away though. For several years, it sat unused in the back, left-hand drawer of his desk. Right now, it was riding along with them in his wallet.

Everybody else seemed so sure about him having sex. Everything he'd ever seen on TV or heard about said it was great. But would she think so? And what about afterwards? Everything might be great, but it would also be different. He just wasn't sure whether it would be worth it.

In yesterday's culture, much sexual behavior was considered socially impermissible. Most people didn't consider engaging in inappropriately sexualized behavior because family, society, and religious training reinforced personal boundaries against such behavior. Today's society leaves people basically on their own to decide what is and is not acceptable behavior. The social barriers have been breached, and sexualized behavior has flooded in.

In order to stem the tide, each person needs to replace those breached social barriers with core beliefs, derived from God's Word and not from the shifting sand of culture. Each person must decide what behavior they will consider "impossible."

What You Will Not Say (Tongue Control)

If you say something, you've thought about it. Ephesians 5:3–4 links action with words: "But among you there must not be even a hint of sexual immorality, or of any kind of impurity, or of greed, because these are improper for God's holy people. Nor should there be obscenity, foolish talk or coarse joking, which are out of place, but rather thanksgiving."

Control your tongue, and you control a major influence of your actions. James knew full well the power of the tongue when he wrote, "The tongue is a small part of the body, but it makes great boasts. Consider what a great forest is set on fire by a small spark. The tongue also is a fire, a world of evil among the parts of the body. It corrupts the whole person, sets the whole course of his life on fire, and is itself set on fire by hell" (3:5–6).

In the words of another simple children's song, "Be careful little tongue what you say; be careful little tongue what you say; there's a Father up above, looking down to show the way, so be careful little tongue what you say."

What You Will Not Do (Hand Control)

In Matthew 5:27–28, God establishes the eye-heart connection mentioned previously. He continues this thought in verses 29 and 30: "If your right eye causes you to sin, gouge it out and throw it away. It is better for you to lose one part of your body than for your whole body to be thrown into hell. And if your right hand causes you to sin, cut it off and throw it away. It is better for you to lose one part of your body than for your whole body to go into hell."

After your eye has viewed it and your heart has condoned it, your hand commits it. In order to hold fast against cultural battering, you need to recognize the steps taken to sexual immorality. Once your eye has viewed it, you have sinned, but you can still stop. Once your heart has condoned it, you have sinned, but you can still stop. Once your hand has committed it, there is no stopping. The deed is done.

"Be careful little hand what you do; be careful little hand what you do; there's a Father up above, looking down with love for you, so be careful little hand what you do."

Where You Will Not Go (Foot Control)

"With persuasive words she led him astray; she seduced him with her smooth talk. All at once he followed her like an ox going to the slaughter, like a deer stepping into a noose till an arrow pierces his liver, like a bird darting into a snare, little knowing it will cost him his life.... Do not let your heart turn to her ways or stray into her paths.... Her house is a highway to the grave, leading down to the chambers of death" (Proverbs 7:21–23, 25, 27).

Often, temptations to sexual sin occur in specific places. We have to make a choice to go there, knowing what could happen if we do. By venturing to a place where we have reason to believe we may be tempted, we are acting without thought of consequence, just like an animal. God made us to be more than animals. He gave us a mind and a will to guide our steps.

It is not fate we tempt when we knowingly enter into a potentially dangerous situation. It is not fate we tempt when we consciously enter into an inappropriately sexualized relationship. It is not fate we tempt; it is sin we commit. As you take your steps in life and in relationships, use the mind of Christ and the will of God to guide you.

"Be careful little feet where you go; be careful little feet where you go; there's a Father up above, looking down and he will know, so be careful little feet where you go."

Where You Will Not Look (Eye Control)

The power of the eye in sexual situations has been identified earlier in Scripture. This is an area where Scripture and culture are in agreement. Culture understands clearly how visual images affect sexual desire. For men, especially, visual sexual stimulation is powerful. King David saw his beautiful neighbor bathing, and that one peek seduced his righteous soul to commit unimaginable sins. He was a clear-cut victim of "the lust of the eyes."

Nowhere is visual stimulation more accessible today than over the Internet. In a *USA Today*/Associated Press/MSNBC poll, reported in the June 22, 1998, issue of *Time* magazine, 50 percent of men who visited sex sites online said they preferred sites with visual erotica compared to only 23 percent who said they preferred chat rooms, where erotica was presented in text form. Purveyors of pornography have always recognized the visual connection to sexual stimulation.

One important way to avoid the temptation of sexualized relationships is to make wise choices about what you decide to view. If, for example, you make it a habit to view pornography, you reinforce in your own heart and mind the notion that all members of the opposite sex exist to be viewed sexually. This can increase your tendency to view coworkers and other associates sexually. Your eye and your heart act together in sin to motivate your own sinful conduct. Circumvent this process by denying your eye opportunity to sin.

"Be careful little eyes where you look; be careful little eyes where you look; there's a Father up above; he knows a look is all it took, so be careful little eyes where you look."

What You Will Not Think (Heart Control)

Jesus said, "Out of the heart come evil thoughts, murder, adultery, sexual immorality, theft, false testimony, slander" (Matthew 15:19).

"From within," Jesus taught, "out of men's hearts, come evil thoughts, sexual immorality, theft, murder, adultery, greed, malice, deceit, lewdness, envy, slander, arrogance and folly. All these evils come from inside and make a man 'unclean'" (Mark 7:21–23).

Thoughts can be notoriously difficult to control. Some people do not see a need to control thoughts at all so long as those thoughts do not translate into action. The problem with this theory is that thoughts are almost sure to become translated into action, especially at times when we are tired or weakened or tempted.

God understands the need to control our thoughts. He knows that our thoughts have a tendency toward evil. He counsels us to fill our minds with good things, thus crowding out the evil we will eventually think. Do you recall the list he gives us in Philippians 4:8? "Whatever is true, whatever is noble, whatever is right, whatever is pure, whatever is lovely, whatever is admirable—if anything is excellent or praiseworthy—think about such things." Good things like these can replace thoughts of sexual immorality.

Have you ever said to yourself that you weren't going to think about something? You decided whatever it was, you just weren't going to think about it anymore. What happened? If you didn't start thinking something else or doing something else, how long was it before you were back to thinking about it again? Didn't take you very long, did it? When powerful sexual temptations try to take over our minds, they can be almost impossible to erase from our consciousness. They stick to our minds like chewing gum to shoes. At such moments we must seek the help of God's Spirit so that we may "take captive every thought to make it obedient to

Christ" (2 Corinthians 10:5). Replace disruptive sexual fantasies with scriptures you have committed to memory for this express purpose. When sinful thoughts arise, block them out by reciting God's word silently until his holiness fills your soul.

"Be careful little heart what you think; be careful little heart what you think; there's a Father up above, if you look or if you blink, so be careful little heart what you think."

HELP FOR TONGUE-HAND-FOOT-EYE-HEART CONTROL

One wise man wrote, "A scoundrel and villain, who goes about with a corrupt mouth, who winks with his eye, signals with his feet and motions with his fingers, who plots evil with deceit in his heart—he always stirs up dissension. Therefore disaster will overtake him in an instant; he will suddenly be destroyed—without remedy" (Proverbs 6:12–15).

The struggle all of us face daily is to control these elements in all aspects of our lives, including our decisions regarding relationships. The consequences of failing to control these elements is obvious from Scripture. But sometimes the combination can be difficult to control, more difficult to handle than we have strength. Luckily, control is not up to our strength alone. We have as a gift from our Father above his very presence, his Holy Spirit, living within us. With this heavenly help, we have the strength we need to rebuild our core beliefs along God's guidelines. When we do this, he will provide the brick and mortar, the stones and grout, through his word and his Spirit, to fortify the truth in our lives.

"So do not fear," he promises, "for I am with you; do not be dismayed, for I am your God. I will strengthen you and help you; I will uphold you with my righteous right hand" (Isaiah 41:10).

—— Fuel for Thought ——

It is important for you to accept God's authority in your life. His precepts are not just good ideas. They are commands. As you answer the following questions in your notebook or binder, be aware of your own feelings regarding God's sovereignty in your life.

1. Look back over the biblical account of David's sin with Bathsheba. Consider how David failed to control his actions concerning her.

2. What cultural messages would David have heard regarding his conduct with Bathsheba? How were those messages in conflict with God's Word?

3. List who or what influences your decisions in life. Now prioritize the list. Who or what has the most influence in your life decisions? (Examples: money, family, friends, God, religious upbringing, personal desires, etc.)

4. As you look back over your life, what have you been building your life on? Have the foundations you've chosen proved to be made of rock or of sand?

5. Read Proverbs 5 through 7. List the number of times God warns against adultery or sexual immorality. What are some of the negative consequences associated with sexual immorality?

6. Using the scriptures you listed or others you have studied, compose your own list of Core Beliefs.

7. In your notebook or binder, write the following headings and answer accordingly:

   a. What I Will Not Say:

   b. What I Will Not Do:

c. Where I Will Not Go:

d. Where I Will Not Look:

e. What I Will Not Think:

MAY GOD BLESS YOUR COMMITMENT *and resolve to follow his paths for your life and relationships. May God continue to reveal his perfect will for your life and relationships.*

THE SATISFACTION
GAINED FROM A
MEETING OF THE
MINDS CAN CAUSE
PEOPLE TO SEEK
OTHER FORMS OF
SATISFACTION.

3

He who guards his mouth and his tongue keeps himself from calamity.
—Proverbs 21:23

RECOGNIZE
THE POWER OF PARTNERING

A Meeting of the Minds
Can Lead to Trouble

Connie knew she had come to the right place. Having just completed her degree in psychology and youth counseling, she was thrilled to be able to work for a large church as an intern. She was glad she was going to be able to put her knowledge to use. The church already had a youth staff of twelve. Most of them were her age, but some were older. Her fondest dream was coming true: to get on this church staff as an intern so she could work up to a permanent position.

Connie loved God, loved kids. She poured herself into the job, ever ready to drop everything and volunteer for whatever needed to be done. To know she was working for a cause to which she could give her heart without reservation gave her a great sense of purpose.

After working at the church for a while, Connie was impressed at how polite the men on staff were to the women who worked there. She detected no machismo, as she had at other organizations. Here the men listened to the women with whom they worked. They took the women seriously and helped them achieve their goals for ministry. Together, the men and women seemed to work as a team, combining their efforts and energy into furthering God's kingdom. To Connie it was truly a slice of heaven.

One evening, the music minister at the church, Richard, asked Connie to help him select some contemporary worship tunes to teach the kids. Richard said he knew it was late but wondered if she could spare half an hour or so. Of course, Connie was more than willing to oblige even though the request came late in the evening after a session with all the staff. She knew the youth conference was coming up shortly and figured Richard needed all the help he could get. She greatly admired his skill and dedication to ministry and was flattered he had asked her to help with such an important job.

The rest of the staff began to file out of the building, leaving Connie and Richard at the keyboard in the music room. As Connie sorted through the pile of music on the side table, she would take out one that caught her interest, and Richard would play it on the keyboard. Together they began to sing. Connie had a strong alto voice, and Richard instinctively took the melody on the songs he played. She enjoyed the sound of their harmony together. By the eighth or ninth measure of each piece, both of them had an idea of whether the song would work.

One by one the rest of the lights in the office darkened, leaving Connie and Richard alone, laughing and working together to pick out their music. Before they realized it, over an hour had passed, and they hastily packed up the piles of sheet music and went home, having accomplished a great deal.

The next morning both Connie and Richard were busy with their individual duties. In the afternoon, however, Richard sought out Connie and asked if she would be free to finish up the work they'd started the previous evening. Connie was more than willing to oblige.

After the rest of the staff left for the day, Connie and Richard returned to the music room to continue what they had started the night before. Again they were all alone. Now more comfortable with each other, Connie and Richard joined to sing about God's compassion. Connie could see the emotion on Richard's face as he sang and talked about God's love. She realized how much she admired Richard for his faith and his work at the church.

Before long they had finished picking out the songs for the conference, but neither of them was eager to go home. Instead, the camaraderie and relaxed atmosphere spilled over from work talk to personal conversations. Richard said he wanted to "reward" Connie for all of her hard work. He invited her to dinner at a local restaurant. Connie had to admit it gave her a warm feeling when Richard graciously insisted on paying for her meal. He said it was "the least" he could do.

As Richard drove her back to her car at church, Connie found herself gazing at Richard's profile. He was a nice looking man with a wonderful smile. Funny, she had never really looked at him before. She did now.

THE POWER OF PARTNERING

Whenever two people partner to accomplish a common goal, a unique relationship is formed. Effort, intensity, time, and togetherness combine in a potent combination, often vital to completing a given assignment. These factors, while combining to complete a task, also create a sense of togetherness. This sense of connection can, in turn, lead to a false sense of intimacy. Unchecked, the satisfaction gained from a meeting of the minds can cause one or both parties to seek other forms of satisfaction from the relationship.

When Efforts Combine

A partnering relationship requires joint effort. The parties involved must combine their efforts to accomplish a common goal. They strive together, brainstorm together, sometimes even sweat together. Often the length of the task requires a give-and-take effort, with one partner switching off with the other as stamina or inspiration swings from person to person. Through this effort swing, each partner learns to trust and rely on the other.

The synergy that combined efforts provide can be truly amazing. The combination of effort results in more work product than either could achieve individually. By joining efforts, two people can work harder, work faster, and accomplish more than either could alone. The multiplying effect of joint effort can lead to the conclusion that something is special or unique in the pairing. Conversely, the conclusion can be drawn that without the other partner, nothing can be achieved. A dependency upon the partnering has then been established.

Adding Intensity

Some partnerships continue over a long period of time, gaining momentum over months and years. Other partnerships are born in time-sensitive circumstances. A job needs to be done quickly. In such pairings a crisis mode takes over, adding intensity to the partnership. They not only have to get the job done; they have to get it done on time.

In an intense, time-pressured partnership, caution may be thrown to the wind. A person who usually leaves the office at a specific time each day may stay late. People who are careful with everything they eat may, while in this crisis mode, gobble down the delivered pepperoni pizza three nights in a row. A person who is careful to keep a respectful distance from a colleague may allow that zone to constrict under the pressure. In the emergency, whether real or created, people may compromise or alter guidelines that normally govern their behavior.

The intensity created in the work situation can mirror the intensity we experience in sexual relationships. The feelings of attachment and unity can be similar enough to cause confusion. Even if the conscious mind does not acknowledge the connection, often the subconscious mind will. One or both of the partners may find themselves suddenly considering the other from a sexual point of view.

It's about Time

Intensive, emergency-oriented tasks can fast-forward relationships from work to personal. While intensity tends to blast through relationship boundaries, time tends to erode those same boundaries. The more time two people spend together, the more comfortable they may become with each other. The more comfortable two people become, the more they share. The more they share, the more they begin to view themselves as a couple, partnered together. They begin to see themselves within a relational context. Coworkers may reinforce this perception of the two being a "couple" by the joint recognition and praise given to the partners for their achievement.

Intense relationships that burst explosively into flame may also burn out quickly. The danger with relationships that evolve slowly over time is their longstanding nature. Such relationships produce no crackle and sizzle, only the smoldering glow of long-burning embers. These entrenched relationships seem to have less tendency to burn out of their own intensity.

In workplace relationships like the ones just described, the time may come when one or the other party will loosen up too much, allowing a boundary to slip. Project partners may eventually allow too much or guard themselves too little in their relationships. An extended-time relationship obviously offers a multitude of opportunities for this to happen. If both partners are not careful to continually reestablish boundaries to keep their relationship within the proper framework, these "slips" can lead to one or the other party beginning to view the partnership as more than it should be.

You and Me against the World

Partners on workplace projects may begin to feel a sense of shared identity for several reasons. If the partnership is time intensive, it's "you and me" against the clock. If the partnership is between peers, it's "you and me" against the boss. If the partnership requires a great deal of effort, it's "you and me" against failure. If the partnership requires a great deal of time, it's "you and me" against burnout. If the partnership requires a truly exceptional work product, it's "you and me" against mediocrity. All of these "you and me" situations can forge a strong joint identity that can subtly overshadow other existing relationships. Indeed, if one of the existing relationships attempts to intervene in the partnership, it could turn into a "you and me" against "them" situation, realigning relationship priorities.

MORE THAN MAKING MUSIC

Over time, Connie and Richard started meeting for coffee. The more intense their friendship became, the more they decided it would be best to conceal it, just so people didn't get any "wrong ideas." After all, Richard was married and Connie wasn't. Sure, they were just meeting in a neutral place to discuss work, but someone might see and misunderstand. So they decided to meet for coffee in a nearby town where the chance of their being spotted together would be less.

Richard began to really look forward to their meetings. He admitted to himself that it was kind of exciting, freeing almost, to drive down the highway to the next town to meet with Connie. At first, they confined their conversations to work. Soon, though, Richard began to tell Connie about his background, his family, his wife. He began to ask her, "from a woman's point of view," to explain some of his wife's behavior. It wasn't long before the behavior they were discussing included highly personal, even sexual, details.

Richard told himself he wasn't doing anything wrong. After all, he and Connie were just talking, nothing more. But their growing partnership began to show up at work in seemingly innocent but unmistakable ways: the casual hug across the shoulders as they left the building together, the relaxed grasping of hands before saying good-bye, the electric jolt both of them felt when they'd see each other unexpectedly during the day.

In late August Connie and Richard spent hours and hours working to pull off a major youth event at church. On the final evening Richard offered Connie a ride home. Her car was in the shop and a friend had brought her to work that morning. Connie accepted, flush with the success of what the two of them had worked so hard to accomplish. Before Richard got to her apartment, he stopped the car on a darkened back street. Switching off the lights, he turned to Connie to thank her, again, for all her hard work and to tell her how much she meant to him.

Gazing at her face, so open, with eyes peering up at his, Richard began to verbalize his appreciation for Connie and ended up showing it instead. Grasping her chin, Richard leaned over and kissed Connie on the mouth. Instantly, he was mortified—until he realized she was kissing him back, enthusiastically. The sexual tension that had been building in their relationship burst forth, and they fell into each other's arms. Every remaining barrier was breached. That night Connie and Richard began a sexual relationship that would end up forcing Connie to leave the church and causing Richard to lose both his job and the trust and love of his family.

PARTNERING AT WORK

One of the primary arenas for male-female interaction in today's world is the workplace. Take a twenty-four-hour day. Subtract the average eight-hour sleep cycle. Subtract travel time. Subtract evening outside activities. Take out the average eight to ten hours a day people spend at their jobs. What is left is at-home, family time. Can you see that many people spend more actual time every week with their colleagues at work than they do with their families? It is a simple fact of life that extensive time together often translates into increasingly sexualized relationships.

Workplace romances can occur in some circumstances more easily than in others. The danger that a work-based relationship will turn sexual greatly increases if both of the parties are single. In today's society, sex between singles carries almost no stigma. If two single people in a workplace decide to carry on a sexual relationship, many employers today do not care, so long as their work product does not suffer. Only if their relationship hinders the bottom line of the business is it a problem. In offices or factories that employ large numbers of singles, who is sleeping with whom may become as complicated as which guy was "going steady" with which girl back in junior high school.

As in the example of Connie and Richard, the potential also exists for an employee who is single to become involved with one who is married, especially if they are partnered together at work. (A subsequent chapter will deal with the dangers inherent for partners of unequal rank.)

The quality of partnering at work can be compelling when compared to some of the partnering that goes on in marriages. Work partnering often focuses on a specific, goal-oriented task. The rewards for the partnered task are also specific and readily identified, such as money, promotions, or benefits. The rewards for marriage partnering are more elusive and long-term, such as raising responsible children or completing distant financial goals. Within a marriage relationship, much of the "work product" can easily be taken for granted. Washing the dishes, folding the laundry, or mowing the lawn generally are not treated with fanfare of any kind.

Unfortunately, the only time the "work product" in most marriages gets noticed is when it is neglected, not when it is accomplished with skill, whereas at work excellence is generally noticed and reacted to. All of this "neglect" at home contrasted with applause at work can make a spouse falsely conclude that he or she is appreciated at work but taken for granted at home, possibly resulting in resentment and a weakening of the boundary of marital fidelity.

In some workplace romances, of course, both parties are married. Two people whose marriages are stale or troubled may be especially vulnerable to the excitement and allure of a "live" relationship. Some may be less afraid of an improper relationship with a married person because the liaison will likely be temporary and, therefore, easier to contain. For some the purpose of the sexualization may have little to do with wanting to establish a permanent relationship and more to do with transitory, sexual gratification.

PARTNERING AT PLAY

After dropping off the kids at school at exactly 8:10 every morning, Janice would climb back into the car, breathe a sigh of relief, put on an Amy Grant cassette, and head off to her early ritual at the local fitness club. It was a routine Janice had come to enjoy. Her husband was at work, her kids were at school, and she finally had an hour to herself. It became the best part of her day.

For the first month or so, it was just Janice and the equipment. She'd sweat for thirty minutes on the treadmill, lift some small weights to tone muscles, and then stretch out the kinks. She found herself snatching quick glances in the mirrors bordering every wall of the health club. She had to admit she was looking pretty good for a married mother of two.

Though she couldn't remember exactly, Janice supposed he'd been there from the first day she joined the club. She just never noticed him, a handsome man, about the age of her husband. He was graying slightly at the temples, tanned, toned, and most attractive.

She remembered one morning he offered to help when she couldn't figure out one of the machines. She had been grateful for his assistance, so she smiled when she saw him there the next day.

He introduced himself and said he was glad they'd met the day before. She told him her name and said she'd see him again. Almost without thinking, she told him how good it was to have a man around the gym. They started talking and worked out together for a full hour the next day, sweating together and getting to know one another. The following day they worked out together again, and the day after that.

Suddenly mornings at the club were more enjoyable than ever. After working out together, Janice and Matt would go down to the juice bar and unwind just talking. Before she knew it her hour workout started stretching to an hour and a half and sometimes two. Small talk became more serious. "We're becoming better friends," Janice told herself.

It wasn't like her to do anything wrong, she thought as she drove home from the gym. He was a new friend. Why couldn't she have a man for a friend? What was wrong with that? They had a lot of things in common. She wasn't doing anything wrong. Just talking.

One day after an especially great time of conversation and being together, Janice was shocked to realize she was beginning to develop strong secret feelings for Matt. At first she tried to deny them because they scared her. But along with the fear was an electric excitement. She felt energized, alive, more than she had for a long time.

The next morning, Janice spent more time than usual putting on her makeup. When she was tempted to stray from her diet, the image of Matt was there and what he'd think about any extra pounds. She began to take more care about other aspects of her body too. Soon, she was dabbing strategic areas of her body with perfume. "No use smelling like a gym," she thought, even though she was in one.

One morning after they'd finished their routine and were cooling down, Matt brought her a cool drink. As he handed it to her, the back of his hand brushed slowly and gently against her breast. A jolt went through Janice from the top of her ponytail to the tips of her toes. It was a feeling she hadn't felt in years. Looking up into his eyes, she knew the touch wasn't accidental. He had meant every second of it. The fact that he found her sexually attractive should have sent Janice running in the other direction. It should have, but it didn't.

Whether at work or at play, we still need to be aware of the potential for any relationship to become sexualized. Recreational activities often take place at a neutral site separated from other relationships. We go there to work out or play basketball or shoot pool. Any person there is identified within the context of that activity. They can exist for that moment apart from any of their other relationships. Young men have no girlfriends. Wives have no husbands. Fathers have no children. Unless these other relationships are valued and established, they are in danger of being sidelined when we step into the artificial, temporary world of a ball field or a gym.

Some people translate the relaxed nature of playtime activities into a time when they can "let their hair down," loosening boundaries or restrictions on behavior. Their very concept of play means no rules. The activity is engaged in to forget responsibilities, not to reinforce them. Such an atmosphere is ripe for allowing a relationship within that zone to become inappropriately sexualized.

PARTNERING ONLINE

Recent technology has presented us with a new, potentially devastating forum for inappropriately sexualized relationships (as explained more fully in the authors' recent book *The Hidden Dangers of the Internet* published by Shaw). The Internet with its anonymity and wide-open content can tempt us to cross physical and sexual boundaries. On the Internet, relationships are formed and reinforced daily over e-mail, on bulletin boards, and in the thousands of chat rooms available for anyone with a modem connection and a little time to spend. Accessibility, anonymity, and lack of accountability on the Internet make it fertile ground for nurturing sexual content.

Over the Internet it is now possible to carry on a sexually explicit, verbal "affair" with another person while you sit in the privacy of your own home with your family watching television in the next room. With just a click of the mouse, you can send your messages to another person. By the use of a private password, you, and only you, can access your e-mail. With just a little bit of care, no one else in your house need know what you are really doing when you stay up until three o'clock in the morning.

Over the Internet you don't have to give out any information about yourself. Your anonymity is complete. Communicate by screen name, refrain from mentioning any physical details about where you live, and no one can find you unless you want to be found. Divulge too much on e-mail, and all you need to do is change your e-mail address. Any inquiries to your old address will come back to whoever sent them as "non-deliverable mail." Over the Internet it is completely possible to keep details of your life private.

Online you can even make up details of your life. The other person has no way to know whether you are telling the truth. The temptation to construct a fantasy personality within which to hide on the Internet seems to be tremendous. Once consigned to fantasy and shielded from accountability for what we write or think, many of our fantasies tend to meld with the sexual. Hidden, anonymous, we can say whatever we really want, and no one will gasp in shock or shake their head at us disapprovingly.

Securely anonymous, many people find themselves conducting conversations over the Internet of a highly personal and, often, sexual nature. Many people log on to the Internet primarily to indulge in sexual parlays. According to the *USA Today*/Associated Press/MSNBC poll reported in the June 22, 1998, issue of *Time* magazine referenced earlier, even though 50 percent of men preferred visual erotica, 49 percent of the women gave chat rooms as their preferred destination for erotic interaction.

Plenty of people online are looking for another person to engage in highly sexual chat-room conversations. Some of these people have become so enamoured of each other that they have actually left spouses to initiate physical relationships with the cyber-lovers they met online.

—————— Fuel for Thought ——————

Priorities have a way of becoming skewed. The urgent transcends the important. The flashy overshadows the ordinary. The mysterious clouds the mundane. Think about the relationships you have and the importance you are giving to them.

1. In your binder or notebook, make a list of your current relationships, both at home and work. Assign the amount of time spent during a typical week within each relationship. How does the time measure up? To which relationship are you giving the most time? Is it the relationship you should be giving the most time to? If not, why not?

2. Have you ever considered a coworker from a sexual point of view? Are you considering one now? If so, who is that person? Write down the name.

3. As you review your current relationships, do you have a sense that you are being pursued by someone at work? Have you found yourself in a compromising situation where you felt uncomfortable?

4. Are you the type of person who enjoys the attention, the approval of members of the opposite sex?

5. Do you enjoy flirting with people you find personally attractive?

It can be difficult to recognize when you have strayed over a boundary and ventured into an inappropriate relationship. It can be difficult to admit that someone else you respect and have trusted is viewing you through a sexual lens. It can be difficult to find the courage to reestablish boundaries, whether it is you or someone else who has neglected those boundaries.

Recognizing a danger is the first step to avoiding it.

MAY GOD BLESS YOUR EFFORT *to bring clarity and integrity to your work and play relationships.*

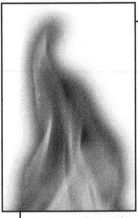

Now Naomi had a relative on her husband's side, a man of standing, whose name was Boaz.

Ruth said to Naomi, "Let me go to the fields and pick up the leftover grain behind anyone in whose eyes I find favor."

Naomi said to her, "Go ahead, my daughter." As it turned out, she found herself working in a field belonging to Boaz.

Just then Boaz arrived and greeted the harvesters, "The LORD be with you!"

"The LORD bless you!" they called back.

Boaz asked the foreman of his harvesters, "Whose young woman is that?"

"She is the Moabitess who came back from Moab with Naomi."

So Boaz said to Ruth, "My daughter, listen to me. Don't go and glean in another field and don't go away from here. Stay here with my servant girls. Watch the field where the men are harvesting, and follow along after the girls. I have told the men not to touch you. And whenever you are thirsty, go and get a drink from the water jars the men have filled."

At mealtime Boaz said to her, "Come over here. Have some bread and dip it in the wine vinegar."

She ate all she wanted and had some left over. As she got up to glean, Boaz gave orders to his men, "Even if she gathers among the sheaves, don't embarrass her. Rather, pull out some stalks for her from the bundles and leave them for her to pick up, and don't rebuke her."

So Ruth gleaned in the field until evening. Then she threshed the barley she had gathered. She carried it back to town, and her mother-in-law saw how much she had gathered.

Her mother-in-law asked her, "Where did you glean today? Where did you work? Blessed be the man who took notice of you!"

"The name of the man I worked with today is Boaz," she said.

"The LORD bless him!" Naomi said to her daughter-in-law. "He has not stopped showing his kindness to the living and the dead." She added, "That man is our close relative; he is one of our kinsman-redeemers. It will be good for you, my daughter, to go with his girls, because in someone else's field you might be harmed."

So Ruth stayed close to the servant girls of Boaz to glean until the barley and wheat harvests were finished.

—from Ruth 2

4

The prudent see
danger and take
refuge, but the simple
keep going and
suffer for it.
—Proverbs 27:12

AVOID
ADDING FUEL TO THE FIRE

Clear Boundaries in
Close Relationships

Charlie was taken completely by surprise. At first, it didn't register through the haze of his confusion. There was no way, though, he could misread the message. Tricia had just flat out asked him to go out together after work. A myriad of thoughts raced through Charlie's brain.

Maybe she didn't mean anything by it. After all, they had spent a lot of time getting the restaurant up and running, ready for the opening. Maybe she thought going out would be a way to get away from things and relax.

Maybe she'd already asked a bunch of the other kitchen crew and he was just one of many. Maybe this was some sort of a group outing and he'd just missed everyone else's being invited. What if he were jumping to a major-league, totally wrong conclusion?

Maybe she hadn't realized he was married. He'd mentioned his wife, his kids, hadn't he? Certainly she knew he went home to a family. Right?

Tricia took his momentary paralysis as acceptance. She moved toward him and taking hold of his arm, drew it in toward her body with her left hand, rubbing the inside of his elbow with her right. She told him about a coffee shop about ten minutes from work that would be just perfect.

Charlie disengaged his arm, stammering that there'd been some sort of a mistake. He was married and, though he was flattered, he didn't think having coffee with Tricia would go over well with his wife.

Tricia responded that the only way for Charlie's wife to know was if Charlie told her. Otherwise, it could remain their little secret.

In a firm voice, Charlie reiterated that he did not intend to have coffee with Tricia. He was married, happily married, and not interested in doing anything that would hurt his wife and their marriage.

Tricia smiled and said that he might not be interested now, but if he ever was, to give her a call. With that, she lazily worked her way out of the restaurant, glancing back at Charlie and smiling as she exited the building.

Only after she'd gone did Charlie realize he was sweating.

KEEP YOUR BOUNDARIES INTACT

Some of you may have concluded from this story that all of the blame for the incident rested on Tricia. After all, she was the one who initiated the contact, right? But think about it a moment. What if Charlie never had mentioned his wife or his family? What if his comments and actions toward Tricia were flirtatious? It is not always possible for us to count on the boundaries of others to keep our relationships from becoming sexualized. Their boundaries may not be at the same place as ours. Or they may have no boundaries for us to rely on at all.

Why all of this talk about boundaries? Because the biological facts are incontestable. Whenever men and women work and play together, sexual attraction will be present. Always. It goes with the territory. When a winsome lass like Ruth appears in the field, the young men get excited. And not every field (or office or factory) is fortunate enough to have a boss like Boaz who made sure the relationships in his work area stayed safe and wholesome. In the modern workplace men and women often get to know each other very, very well. This familiarity can allow boundaries to slip. Likewise, the informal nature of recreational activities allows our inhibitions and boundaries to be relaxed. Confusion arises when people misconstrue closeness in work or play as intimacy.

Set Your Boundaries Ahead of Time

Since all male-female partnering relationships have the potential for becoming sexualized, we need to enter these relationships in a wise manner. Our actions and decisions regarding how we conduct ourselves within these relationships can affect their eventual outcome. The time to make those decisions is before we enter into any relationship, for our ability to think clearly may be compromised later by the situation or the individual. Set boundaries ahead of time.

Boundaries are helpful in two ways. First, they define actions and behaviors we will not allow from others toward us. In this way, boundaries act as barriers against others' inappropriate behavior. Second, boundaries set parameters for actions and behaviors we will not permit ourselves to engage in. Boundaries act like guardrails, keeping us from careening off the correct course and into areas of danger.

Use Boundaries to Reduce Embarrassment

Additionally, having clearly established boundaries allows us to remove the personal component from highly charged situations. Having to confront sexualized behavior can be embarrassing. So embarrassing that some people would rather give in to the behavior, hoping that if they ignore it, it will go away. We can minimize this embarrassment by explaining our boundaries if someone of the opposite sex steps across one of them. The focus, then, is not their behavior but our boundary. Thus we may be able to depersonalize the situation and rob it of some of its embarrassment.

Simply saying, "I make it a point never to go out to lunch alone with guys from the office," may keep a female coworker from having to deal with a potentially difficult situation. The boundary can be stated inoffensively, the implication being, "It's nothing personal. These are just my rules." In the embarrassment of an improperly sexual situation, having simple boundaries to fall back on when our minds have fuzzed over can be quite helpful.

BOUNDARY #1: KEEP RELATIONSHIPS CLEAR

Within relationships fuzziness is not a plus. Fuzzy boundaries can lead to fuzzy relationships, where neither party is exactly sure how much the other person is willing to put into the relationship. Fuzzy relationships create sexual confusion when one person creates an assumption out of the vacuum of unexpressed boundaries. "Be...alert," the Scriptures warn us, for Satan loves to use muddled situations like this to ensnare us. He is constantly on the prowl looking for his next victim (1 Peter 5:8).

When an existing relationship becomes inappropriately sexualized, one or both of the parties lose focus of the original purpose of the partnering. Sexual attraction becomes the prominent motivation for continuing the relationship. At some point, the reason the two people formed the partnership in the first place gets lost or subordinated. The first boundary we must establish for male-female relationships is this: Keep the relationship in context at all times. Why this constant vigilance? Because evil has a tendency to creep up on us unannounced.

If you are in a working relationship with someone of the opposite sex, that relationship exists to fulfill a work function. The reason the two of you are together is because of your work relationship. This is the basis for all of your interaction. Work, in this context, can be employment at a job or involvement in a nonworking task where an end product is desired, such as a political campaign or a civic club project. In these situations, the reason the other person is partnered with you is to complete certain tasks and to interact from a specific perspective. You are fortunate if you get to work with someone you like and respect. Keeping the purpose of your relationship clear, however, will help if your respect and affection for your coworker begins to mutate into sexual affection or feelings of intimacy.

If you are in a play relationship, the purpose of the relationship is obviously to engage in a recreational activity. Sex is never to be viewed as a merely recreational activity, no matter what the media might portray. The goal of most recreational activities is to de-stress, to have fun, and generally, to leave complicated things behind. Getting into a sexual relationship with someone in your club or team is one way to severely complicate your simple leisure time. It has a way of turning the clear into the convoluted, easily and quickly.

Keeping the relationship clear cuts down on the confusion often generated between the two sexes, who often tend to communicate differently. The clearer the relationship, the less chance of an assumption or misunderstanding on the part of one or both parties.

BOUNDARY #2: KEEP RELATIONSHIPS CLEAN

The Bible plainly teaches us that God considers unwholesome speech and coarse joking to be inappropriate in any situation. This is especially true in relationships between men and women. "An evil man is trapped by his sinful talk, but a righteous man escapes trouble" (Proverbs 12:13). A coarse joke, a sexual innuendo, a phrase with a dual, sexual meaning all introduce sexual thoughts into a relationship. Do you think old Boaz's attempt to protect Ruth would have worked if she had flirted with his workers and led them on with loose, crude conversation? Once introduced, sexual talk can promote lustful thinking. Once lust has a foothold in the mind, the other party is viewed through the lens of sexual desire. Jesus says when you do this, you have sinned already without any physical act of infidelity.

We live in an information age and one of its major tenets is "whatever can be known should be known." With the proliferation of television networks, cable networks, Internet news features, magazines, and periodicals, more and more people are devoting themselves to finding out about everything. The tendency in close relationships is to follow the world's model. However, in some relationships, transparency in all areas is not a positive feature. And emotional vulnerability is not a character trait which should be broadcast on all relationship channels. Personal, sexual details of our lives and intimate feelings and desires are not proper content for many relationships. Discretion should always be used in what we share and with whom we share.

The closer a relationship becomes, the deeper the conversation. The deeper the conversation, the more personal information to be divulged. If we continue divulging personal information, we eventually will end up sharing sexual content. This is why close relationships must include constant vigilance in guarding the tongue. We should never be required to share personal and private information with anyone outside of our families. Even within the family, the husband-and-wife relationship remains paramount, with children shielded from information parents are privy to. In the arenas where we work and play, everything that can be known should not be shared.

Especially is this true when we fire up our personal computers and go online. As discussed before, online relationships increase our danger of exposing more private thoughts and preferences than would be wise to share. Sharing personal and sexual information online can almost be like an information auction. If one person shares something private, a secret about themselves, the other person feels duty-bound to reciprocate. The natural urge is to make the next tidbit even more revealing than the first. Each person, in essence, ups the ante or increases the bid with ever more private revelations. In this game of exposure, no one wants to admit they've gone too far. Besides, the voyeuristic nature of people makes such frank confessions quite titillating. For some this familiarity-exchange is akin to foreplay. It excites and sexually stimulates. Participants confess that it also can become habit forming. Online relationships should be approached with extreme caution.

Whether we're online or face to face, experience shows that avoiding overly personal or sexual conversations allows each of the parties to remain focused on the purpose of the relationship. So Boundary #2—keeping our relationships *clean*—is one way to fortify Boundary #1—keeping our relationships *clear*.

BOUNDARY #3: KEEP RELATIONSHIPS ON NEUTRAL GROUND

It was all the computer's fault, actually. If the computer setup at campaign headquarters had been better, Jim never would have suggested that he and Tracy go to his place to work on the leaflet. But the computer at campaign headquarters was donated by someone who had obviously upgraded. It was old and slow and had pitiful memory capacity. His swank publishing program wouldn't even load on it, so Jim suggested they go to his place to work. He was quite proud of his system, and Tracy knew about and liked computers. She was excited to come up and see it. At the time, he didn't realize his computer was the current rendition of "Why don't you come up and view my etchings?"

When she first came into his apartment, she laughed and teased him about his housekeeping skills, or lack thereof. His ears perked up a bit when she quipped that his place lacked a woman's touch. Both of them, then, huddled close to the screen to work on the leaflet. While they waited for a copy to print, he found himself telling Tracy about Susan and why that whole thing hadn't worked out. Tracy seemed sympathetic and shared bits of her latest romantic debacle. They laughed about their common bad luck with the opposite sex.

With a couple of hours of desktop-publishing brilliance, Tracy and Jim created a truly remarkable leaflet. Even the candidate himself thanked them for their hard work. His staff decided they should do all of the leaflets and mail-outs from then on. Pleased with their own creative synergy, they agreed, and began spending more and more time together at Jim's place.

After several weeks of working together, Jim and Tracy were taking a break, sitting together on the couch. Jim stretched out his arms to work the aches and pains out of his neck when Tracy suggested she give him a backrub. One thing led to another and before he knew it, he was lying on the floor with Tracy astride his back, kneading his tired muscles.

It felt great. Everything about it felt great. Tracy was great. Everything about Tracy was great.

When they finally disengaged and stood up, it seemed like touching each other was the most natural thing in the world. Taking Tracy in his arms, Jim continued the physical togetherness they had already started. They were relaxed. The couch was there. It felt like the right thing to do. Neither of them had the strength to stop.

Jim and Tracy's relationship might never have turned sexual if they had wisely insisted on working only at a safe site. An important boundary for all of us to remember is to conduct relationships on neutral ground. Neutral ground means no "your place or mine." When a relationship that should include personal distance between the two partners is conducted at the home of one or both of the parties, the familiarity and seclusion of the surroundings can translate into a loosening of boundaries. The ensuing pattern is then tragically predictable. Familiarity breeds a sense of greater togetherness, which can create a false sense of intimacy, possibly culminating in actual intimacy.

This does not mean coworkers should never set foot in each other's homes. This can happen at legitimate social events such as dinners or holiday parties. The difference with these events, however, is that they are designed for groups of people. In other words, say no to intimate dinners for two, but go ahead and attend the annual staff Christmas party at Fred's place.

One way to honor the neutral ground boundary is to avoid any places and situations where other boundaries may have a tendency to slip. Going out for dinner after the game with your mixed softball team is fine. You're with a large group of people, probably with family members of the team present. You are surrounded by a lot of people who know you. The purpose of the dinner is to continue the camaraderie of the team. The atmosphere of the gathering is open and accessible. Boundaries stay intact in such a setting.

But going out to a steakhouse after work with an opposite-sex colleague in the next office is not fine. The two of you are alone in a darkened room surrounded by people who don't know you, even if they could see well enough to get a good look at you. The purpose of such a get-together is to get together, to promote union. The atmosphere of the meeting is intimate and private. Boundaries have a way of receding in dark, secret, romantic places.

Generally you should have a clear idea of what you consider to be neutral ground. For some, the office of a coworker ceases to be neutral as soon as the door is closed. For others, neutral ground stops at a five-foot radius around a certain individual. People and situations send out "vibes." Listen to your inner voice. It is God-directed and can alert you to situations you should have nothing to do with. So be smart. Interact with opposite-sex associates only on safe, neutral ground. "The highway of the upright avoids evil," the wise man wrote. "He who guards his way guards his life" (Proverbs 16:17). As Scripture says, guard your relationships and you'll protect your life.

BOUNDARY #4: KEEP RELATIONSHIPS FOCUSED OUTWARD

Another way to keep your work and play relationships in perspective is to be aware of the other relationships each of you has. Very few people exist without family. You are someone's mother, daughter, sister, brother, son, or father. Family relationships, especially marriage relationships, have precedence over all others. In God's hierarchy of human relationships, marriage holds center stage, followed by parent-child relationships, extended family relationships, deep friendships, and working relationships. All relationships matter to God. He is even concerned with how we treat strangers and travelers. But some relationships matter far more than others. If we ignore this truth, we always get hurt.

If you are married, you have an obligation to both God and your spouse to keep all your outside relationships from becoming sexualized. If you are single, you have an obligation to your heavenly Father to obey his word regarding any relationship you enter into. In case you have somehow missed it, his word says, "No Spouse—No Sex."

Of course, the primary relationship in the lives of Christians is our relationship to God. After all, Jesus says the greatest commandment given is to "love the Lord your God with all your heart and with all your soul and with all your mind" (Matthew 22:37). "Commit to the LORD whatever you do, and your plans will succeed" (Proverbs 16:3). Every relationship we enter into must be governed by our overriding relationship to him.

Work relationships, as we have seen, can be taken out of their proper context. They can become intense and close, but they must never supersede the other more important relationships in our lives. In our culture today this message has become muddled. We live in a society where other relationships often are subordinated to work relationships and to work itself. People tend to be defined by what they do as opposed to who they are. The worth of an individual is often determined by how much they make at their jobs. Families are uprooted by work-related moves. Many spouses spend evenings alone while their mates work late. Because of work pressures children are expected to hit home runs, dance in recitals, toot trumpets, and receive awards without the presence of a proud parent. Should we be surprised that a host of deluded souls believe that work and work relationships are more important than family?

In our self-centered society, play relationships often are promoted above family. Spouses and children are expected to give up time at home while softball practices and multiple games go on night after night. Being able to stop after work to shoot a round or two of pool or to have a drink with the girls is considered a right by many. Missing breakfast or dinner with family is acceptable in many homes if the absentee is running or biking or working out at the gym. In today's culture our needs have to be met. Our desires take precedence. Our self-esteem dictates that we indulge in whatever activities make us feel good, even if those activities cut us off from the rest of our families.

God never intended our lives to be like this. Our responsibility to nurture our families emotionally and spiritually as well as physically is clearly taught in God's word. The apostles taught that we are worse than pagans if we don't supply the needs of our own families (1 Timothy 5:8). When we are scheduling work or leisure-sports relationships, we need to make sure that our family relationships come first.

————— Fuel for Thought —————

You have seen how important it is for you to have the proper boundaries in your life. God has provided the building blocks in his word for you to wisely construct these proper boundaries. But while God has provided the building blocks, our wrong attitudes and unwise behavior can be the wrecking ball that batters and breaks those boundaries. It is important for us to understand both how God wants us to build these boundaries and how we may weaken them in our own lives.

1. Copy the list of current relationships you made in question 1 at the end of chapter 1. Revise it if it has changed. Beside each, give the purpose of that relationship. Give thought to each relationship and be honest about whether you are expecting more from the relationship than it should give.

2. Be honest and think about the number of conversations you have had that have contained sexual content. Do you enjoy laughing at the latest "dirty joke"? Do you engage in sexually explicit talk when discussing a television show or current events?

3. Ruth's reputation was known to Boaz. Explain how his knowledge of her character and conduct contributed to his actions toward her.

4. What does sexual attraction from the opposite sex do for you? Write down the emotions you feel when you realize someone of the opposite sex finds you attractive.

5. If you have ever found yourself in a compromising situation where you have ventured away from neutral ground, list any warning signs you should have seen before the situation arose. Why did you ignore them?

6. If you stayed away from a compromising situation, list any

warning signs you saw and explain why you paid attention to them.

7. List three reasons why each family member is valuable to you.

8. Within your work environment, do you make it a point to present yourself within your family context? Do you have pictures of your spouse and/or children in your workspace? Do you bring them up in casual conversations with others?

9. If you have discovered that you rarely present yourself in the context of your existing relationships, what do you believe you are trying to accomplish by doing this? Is it important to you to present yourself as autonomous? Does this make you feel more in control of your life?

10. Some people feel that living within boundaries limits their free will. They view this as restrictive. How do you feel about this?

11. What boundaries do you feel you need to maintain at all cost?

12. What boundaries do you need to shore up, boundaries that have fallen into a state of disrepair?

13. What boundaries need to be torn down because they keep you from a deeper relationship with God?

Whether we choose to acknowledge it, all of us live within boundaries. Corporeal boundaries limit where and when we can go and do certain things. Just try going eighty on the freeway past a police officer, and you'll run head-on into a speed limit. Emotional boundaries limit how we can relate to other people. All of us have met people who push these limits to the edge. They are rude, abrasive, and hard to deal with. God the Father has established spiritual boundaries to keep our lives from being ravaged by sin. All of us struggle daily with these spiritual boundaries.

Helpful Resource: If you realize you have an entrenched problem with setting the correct boundaries in your life, consider reading *Boundaries* by Dr. Henry Cloud and Dr. John Townsend, published by Zondervan. This book covers more than sexual boundaries and provides guidelines for how to have healthy physical, mental, emotional, and spiritual boundaries.

MAY GOD GRANT YOU INSIGHT *as you think about the boundaries you have in your life.*

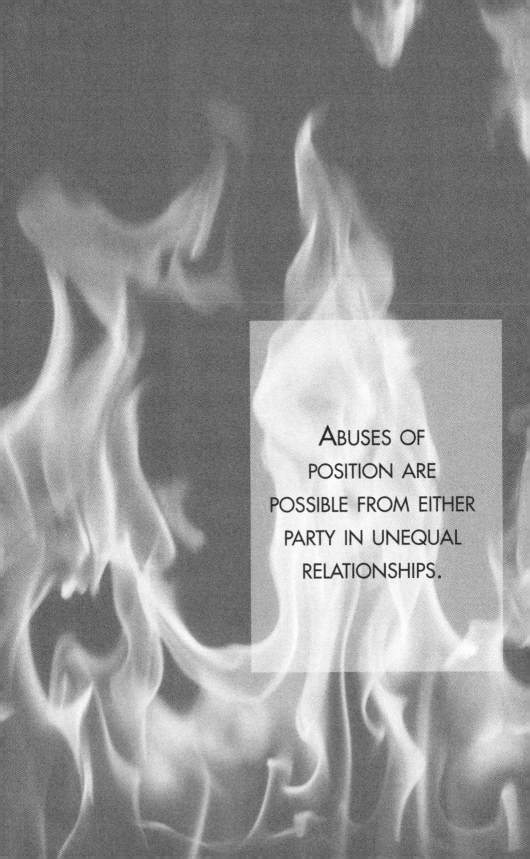

ABUSES OF
POSITION ARE
POSSIBLE FROM EITHER
PARTY IN UNEQUAL
RELATIONSHIPS.

5

Many curry favor
with a ruler, and
everyone is the
friend of a man
who gives gifts.
—Proverbs 19:6

RECOGNIZE
THE POWER OF POSITION

Unbalanced Relationships
Can Make Us Fall

Sheila sat on her bed and cried out in frustra-
tion. What was she going to do? The fear
she'd been carrying around inside for the past six months finally was
realized. He'd made it clear that if she wanted to get her promotion,
she'd have to "cooperate" with him. Sheila had no delusions about
what that cooperation would entail. Either she slept with him or her
promotion was nowhere.

She told him it was sexual harassment and illegal. Prove it, he'd
said. It was just her word against his. He could write up her reviews
any way he wanted. If she cooperated, he'd make sure her next
review was stellar, which was just what he expected out of her performance. The way he'd looked her up and down made it clear it
wasn't her work performance he was referring to.

The whole confrontation, in the privacy of his office, of course,
left Sheila feeling lightheaded and shaky. Now she sat on her bed
and cried and tried to think what to do. She could report his actions
to another supervisor. She'd even threatened him with that. He said
he'd deny it and might even say she propositioned him. Everyone

71

knew she was a single mom trying to raise two young kids while her deadbeat ex-husband kept ducking out of his child-support payments. Everyone knew, he said, her money was tight. Why, there was no telling what desperate measures she might resort to in order to ensure she got the promotion. The way he'd said it made her skin crawl. Even though she knew it wasn't true, he'd made it sound so convincing.

She could look for another job. But this was her first good paying job in two years. Yes, money was tight, but at least there was money. The kids were settled at school and daycare. The benefits at this job were far and away better than any she'd had before. Why, she even had vision care. She didn't want to look for another job. She wanted to keep this one.

She could give in and give him what he wanted. Though he never touched her, not once, while he made his proposal, he kept looking at her and telling her how much he wanted her. After all, he said, she hadn't had a man for, what, at least four years? Didn't she miss the strong arms of a man around her? Didn't she miss the warmth of companionship he could give her? It was really for her benefit, too, and not just the job. That was nothing, really. He made it clear to Sheila that he would be generous in both his physical affection and his acts of appreciation. In fact, the happier he was with her performance, the more he'd make sure she was rewarded.

The office had gotten very warm about that time. Sheila hated herself for wiping at the perspiration that had rolled down her cheek. He'd seen the gesture and smiled. She could smell his cologne and feel the heat as he walked behind her chair and laid his hands on the sides, leaning over her right shoulder. Yes, he'd said, the whole situation could work out to both of their benefits. He'd give her some time to think about it, but not too long.

Closing her eyes against the tears, she realized part of the panic she felt was because, at the end, she'd been tempted to accept right then and there. So much of what he'd said was true. Even now, she could still smell his cologne.

USING SUPERIOR POSITION
TO GAIN SEXUAL CONTROL

Not all relationships are formed on an equal footing. In many, one person will exercise power and authority over the other, and the person in the position of authority may attempt to use that advantage in areas not rightly theirs to control. The subordinate person sometimes may attempt to balance the disparity by initiating a sexual component into the relationship. Abuses of position are possible from either party in unequal relationships.

A person who would attempt to use a superior position to obtain sexual favors from a subordinate could be described as a sexual manipulator. People like this are sexually aggressive, and their objective usually is their own sexual gratification. They have no concern for the best interests of the other person. They tend to be driven by their own fantasies and their own need for sexual control as they manipulate and take advantage of the fearful or confused. Power, prestige, and sexual prowess are their weapons. Their victims are many.

Unfortunately, as this book is being written, America is seeing this scenario being played out in the national media. It started with a young Arkansas state worker who accused then-candidate Bill Clinton of exposing himself to her and requesting sexual favors while he was still governor of Arkansas. According to the testimony of this young woman, he thought because of his position and hers that she should have no problem acceding to his request for a sex act. In her efforts to gain an apology from President Clinton and to seek his public admission of guilt, Paula Corbin Jones instituted a lawsuit against him for sexual harassment.

In the course of this lawsuit a deposition was taken. During questioning by Jones's lawyers, a name was raised along with a question: Had the president ever had sexual relations with a young White House intern named Monica Lewinsky? The attorneys were attempting to show a pattern of sexual predation by the president toward females who were subordinate to him. Eventually the president admitted on national television and in congressional impeachment hearings to having an "inappropriate" relationship with the intern.

This situation forced the country to confront an all-too-familiar scenario: an older, powerful man using his position to obtain sexual favors from a younger, subordinate female. This type of behavior has been branded as sexual harassment in other circumstances. But people seem reluctant to make this charge against the president of the United States. Meanwhile, the question of what is and what isn't sexual harassment fuels vigorous debates.

One temptation of power is to presume a greater scope of that power than is justified. Some people whose position of power and authority makes them able to dictate the actions of the others find the temptation to use that power to require sexual favors compelling. If the person in control is a sexual predator as well as a sexual manipulator, the outcome can be disastrous.

The most amoral of these sexual predators do not concern themselves with legality. In order to be sexually sated, they will rape or molest their object of desire. They will stealthily pursue a victim and manipulate events so that they are able to physically dominate and control the other person. In the most tragic cases, after their sexual satiation, they will injure or kill their victims.

The number of violent sexual predators is, thankfully, low. But there are a greater number of sexual manipulators, who stop short of bodily coercion. Instead of physical force, they use wit, charm, and verbal adeptness to manipulate their intended victims. They chose their targets carefully, being sure of their ability to control events and manipulate that person to get what they desire.

Sexual manipulators tend to be highly competitive individuals. They view most situations as "win or lose." They can be highly driven, focused, and ruthless competitors in other aspects of their lives—characteristics often applauded in the business and secular world. To such personalities, winning is not just important. Winning is everything. Even if the competition in question is sexual in nature. Manipulators are accustomed to having things their way.

With the sexual manipulator, pursuit can be lengthy. Each encounter that produces a small concession on the part of the person under their control fuels their desire and escalates their behavior. They may begin pursuit with overly personal comments about attire or appearance. These innocuous comments may then be followed by increasingly specific, sexual references. These may begin with sexual jokes or comments used to gauge the reactions of the other person. As the manipulator's behavior gradually becomes more sexually overt, the sensibility of the target may be calloused. Each excuse for misbehavior deadens the shock of the next act.

Through all of this behavior, the typical manipulator is smart enough and eloquent enough to easily deflect any initial resistance or objection to their overtures. Often they will create explanations and excuses for their conduct, projecting the blame for any misunderstanding onto their intended target. The more off-guard they can make their target and the more confused their target becomes, the better the atmosphere for the sexual manipulation. Exploiting naiveté, inexperience, uncertainty, and confusion is their game. These responses can actually excite the sexual manipulator. Since most of us are not completely comfortable dealing with the sexual advances of others, sexual manipulators have a built-in advantage, which they use to achieve their selfish goals.

Using Sexual Control
to Gain a Superior Position

Jessica smiled to herself; everything was going according to plan. She'd plotted her strategy like a commander engaged in a battle she had every intention of winning. Her objective was nothing less than becoming Mrs. Jason Peters. The fact there already was a Mrs. Peters was inconsequential: She'd seen the woman. Mr. Peters didn't realize it yet, but his life was about to change. Just about the right time for it too. Jason was a few years past his fortieth birthday and had been married almost twenty years. Jessica planned to have at least the next ten.

The opening skirmish had taken place when she applied for the executive assistant position. Right away, she'd ascertained that Jason was an acceptable objective for her considerable talents and ambitions. That had been over eight months ago, and his delight with her competency at work was evident. They worked together well as a team. Each accomplishment further cemented their working relationship.

For the first several months, Jessica had been sure to keep her distance. During this time she made his likes and dislikes her course of study. By now she knew how he liked his coffee, which types of her attire he was sure to notice, how to read his moods, when he wanted to be all business, and when he wanted to relax. She prided herself in her responsive coloring. Chameleon-like, she read his reactions and responded with whatever she knew he would find most agreeable. She meant to make herself fit him perfectly. So perfectly, in fact, he'd begin to think he couldn't live without her.

At that point, she'd turn up the heat.

The counterpart to the sexual manipulator is the sexual climber. The climber's goal is not merely sexual gratification, unlike the manipulator. The climber's goal is to obtain all of the rights, privileges, power, and position to be gained by aligning themselves with their target. With the manipulator, sex is the goal. With the climber, sex is just a rung in the ladder, the means to elevate position.

The sexual desires of intended targets are secondary to manipulators. Their main goal is their own sexual gratification. If their target is also gratified, fine, but this is not the goal. With the sexual climber, however, the sexual desires of their intended target are of utmost importance, for it is through satisfying those desires that the climber can enhance his or her position.

Like manipulators, sexual climbers can also be in it for the long haul, at least until they target someone else who offers them a step up to a better position. If the intended target does not harbor any sexual desires regarding them, the sexual climber's task is to create those desires. They do so over time, by inserting themselves deeper and deeper into the life and mind of the target.

Successful sexual climbers often move from target to target, climbing highter with each conquest. Skillful climbers can devastate their targets because they so completely overwhelm a person. By shaping themselves to fit their target so well, they totally take over their target's life, crowding out commitments such as family. But once they have gained the advantage through the relationship, the climber may not be content to stay at that level on the ladder. If they have opportunity, they will transfer their affections to a new target, leaving their previous objective crushed in their upward pursuit. Having traded everything of value for a climber, previous targets are left with nothing when the climber moves on.

Because the objective of the sexual climber is not merely sex, when they leave a relationship, they often will take anything of value they can get. Money, goods, friends, and business contacts can all be confiscated by a climber. The destruction they leave in their wake can be staggering to behold.

WHEN MANIPULATORS AND CLIMBERS COLLIDE

Andrew was almost willing to admit that he'd met his match. Several had tried over the last twelve years, but no one nearly as good as Donna. Oh, yes, Andrew had to admit, she was good. Very much in control. He still wasn't sure which of them would win. It made the pursuit that much more exciting.

Working at a small, local college was the perfect environment for Andrew. He immensely enjoyed the adoration of the opposite sex. He never did seem to do as well with other men. They were more product oriented, more "what have you done for me lately." He'd figured out early on he just wasn't cut out for the corporate world. He didn't seem to be able to talk his way out and up as successfully there. Academia was the perfect environment for him.

It was only later that he realized how perfect. All of those young coeds, eager to learn. Andrew was more than eager to share. He was still boyish looking. He kept his body in shape and his hair long. His attire ran to faded blue jeans, white cotton shirt, corduroy jacket, and shoes with no socks. He taught English lit classes, which gave him access to a swarm of idealistic, romantic young women.

That's just the way he liked them. The more idealistic and romantic they were, the easier they were to dismiss afterward. Lines filled with remorse about lives to lead, opportunities to take, and diverging paths allowed him to let them down easily, usually without too much of a scene. For the most part, he could still smile and wave on campus to the ones he'd dumped. Even if not, students usually didn't stay around for long.

Not that he scored every time he went to bat. But he got on base enough of the time to make his career exciting. At least a third of the new freshmen were required to take his beginning English class. Those he didn't have, he still observed on campus. The really attractive young women had a tendency to stand out, although those weren't the ones he usually went for. He preferred the girls who were attractive in a low-key way. The ones who tended to under-play their sexuality. Andrew found it delightful to cause some of those "wallflowers" to "bloom."

Donna was no wallflower. Andrew normally wouldn't have attempted anything with her because of her aggressive, self-confident nature. The battle of wills usually just wasn't worth it. She was the type to cry "Rape!" the next morning. The field was so wide open that Andrew usually didn't tempt fate with someone like Donna. Usually, but not this time.

Donna was a gifted student—when she did her work. This had started the dance, as it turned out. Andrew had called her into his office the semester before to discuss her talent and the lack of turned-in assignments. She'd explained she was a very busy young woman who didn't seem to have the time to complete all of the homework on schedule. She had turned in enough for Andrew to know she could do the work. Why, she asked, did she need to do all of that busy work when she could be devoting herself to other, more productive pursuits?

He'd asked her what was so important that it kept her from her schoolwork. He couldn't remember what she'd said, but he vividly remembered what she was wearing. He remembered in great detail how she'd moved her body around in that chair in his office, adver-tising her assets to their fullest potential. She thanked him for his interest in her and suggested he might be a perfect candidate for her academic advisor. She certainly would be grateful if he'd take a per-sonal interest in her, she said.

He had, and she was. It remained to be seen which of them would come out on top.

When manipulators and climbers collide, the results can be colossal. Each feeds into what the other wants, and both are deter-mined to win the match. While the tendency may be to shrug and say that the two deserve each other, because of the intensity of the combatants, these tainted relationships can produce tragic collateral damage. Family and friends often bear the brunt of the fallout of manipulator-climber collisions. Family gets left on the sidelines of the battle, often sacrificed in the heat of combat. Friends may be called upon to choose sides and can be used as pawns to advance the cause, even if they would prefer to remain conscientious objectors.

——— Fuel for Thought ———

Coming into contact with either a sexual manipulator or a sexual climber is, at best, an unpleasant experience. Most of us tend to minimize our negative experiences, ignoring or rationalizing them. Having to deal with them in this chapter may have left you angry and upset.

You could also have a problem with this chapter about sexual manipulators or climbers if you are one. Your desire to deny the reality of your actions could be causing you to be angry or upset right now.

Don't allow your personal discomfort to keep you from continuing through the materials that follow. Be honest with yourself and forge ahead.

1. As you were reading the case studies in this chapter, did one hit close to home? Which character did you most closely identify with? Were you the manipulator, the climber, or one of their targets?

2. Have you ever used your sexuality in a work or personal relationship to gain a favorable position?

3. Look at your past behavior around members of the opposite sex. Do you have a tendency to use your sexuality to influence them? Describe a time when you used your sexuality to gain a superior position.

4. What are your attitudes toward members of the opposite

sex? Do you consider them compatriots or adversaries? Do you have any simple friendships with members of the opposite sex? Do you have any deep friendships with members of the same sex?

5. List the relationships you have in which you are in a position of authority over others.

6. List the relationships you have in which you are in a position of subordination to others.

7. Is there a difference in the way you respond to the two groups in questions 5 and 6 as far as your sexuality is concerned? If so, how?

8. Name someone in your past or present who has operated as a sexual manipulator. What damage have you seen because of that person?

9. Name someone in your past or present who has operated as a sexual climber. What damage have you seen because of that person?

10. If the person is you, what damage have you experienced because of your behavior?

Admitting that our behavior shows a pattern of deliberate deceit is not easy. We want to minimize our inappropriate behavior as out of character or stress related or just a one-time thing. Our capacity for denial can be enormous.

If you see yourself in this chapter's descriptions of either the sexual manipulator or the sexual climber, you need to know that both of these behavior patterns are destructive personally. They are also changeable. Identifying the pattern is the first step to ending it and adopting a healthy pattern of relationships with the opposite sex.

Deeply entrenched patterns may need to be addressed with the help of a trained professional. Those patterns have a foothold in your past. That past will need to be filtered by someone trained to know what questions to ask and how to advise you during the process. If you had a drug habit, you would seek a drug counselor to help you overcome your addiction. If you had a compulsion to steal, you would seek the help of a therapist to overcome that compulsion. If you are a sexual manipulator or a sexual climber, you have a compulsion to act out sexually in specific and destructive ways. You need to seek the help of a competent counselor or therapist to help you overcome your behavior.

You also need to consider if your deeply entrenched personality patterns set you up to be the target of manipulators or climbers. As you have read this chapter, you may have realized that all too frequently you are finding yourself in that role. If so, somewhere along the line you have adopted the attitudes and reactions of a target. If your behavior has made you vulnerable to either the climber or the manipulator, you also need to seek help to determine why. Manipulators and climbers are only successful when they find willing targets. If you keep being targeted, you should explore why with a trained professional.

Helpful Resources: For a full discussion of sexual harassment, see the book *Sexual Harassment No More* by Jim Conway and Sally Conway from InterVarsity Press.

If you are confused about where to begin to look for help, consider contacting our Web site (www.aplaceofhope.com). There you can ask questions, get a response, and download some additional handouts and articles that could help you. As you look at your relationships and confront unhealthy patterns, you may want to download information we have available on how to build healthy relationships. If we can assist you, please contact us at The Center.

MAY GOD BLESS YOUR DECISION *to seek help for destructive, personal behaviors. May his love remind you of his forgiveness of the sin in your life. May his peace calm your inner turmoil.*

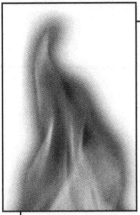

Now Joseph had been taken down to Egypt. Potiphar, an Egyptian who was one of Pharaoh's officials, the captain of the guard, bought him from the Ishmaelites who had taken him there.

When his master saw that the LORD was with him and that the LORD gave him success in everything he did, Joseph found favor in his eyes and became his attendant. Potiphar put him in charge of his household, and he entrusted to his care everything he owned. The blessing of the LORD was on everything Potiphar had, both in the house and in the field. So he left in Joseph's care everything he had; with Joseph in charge, he did not concern himself with anything except the food he ate.

Now Joseph was well-built and handsome, and after a while his master's wife took notice of Joseph and said, "Come to bed with me!"

But he refused, "With me in charge," he told her, "my master does not concern himself with anything in the house; everything he owns he has entrusted to my care. No one is greater in this house than I am. My master has withheld nothing from me except you, because you are his wife. How then could I do such a wicked thing and sin against God?" And though she spoke to Joseph day after day, he refused to go to bed with her or even be with her.

One day he went into the house to attend to his duties, and none of the household servants was inside. She caught him by his cloak and said, "Come to bed with me!" But he left his cloak in her hand and ran out of the house.

When she saw that he had left his cloak in her hand and had run out of the house, she called her household servants. "Look," she said to them, "this Hebrew has been brought to us to make sport of us! He came in here to sleep with me, but I screamed. When he heard me scream for help, he left his cloak beside me and ran out of the house."

She kept his cloak beside her until his master came home. Then she told him this story: "That Hebrew slave you brought us came to me to make sport of me. But as soon as I screamed for help, he left his cloak beside me and ran out of the house." When his master heard the story his wife told him, saying, "This is how your slave treated me," he burned with anger. Joseph's master took him and put him in prison, the place where the king's prisoners were confined.

—from Genesis 39

6

Like a city whose
walls are broken
down is a man who
lacks self-control.
—Proverbs 25:28

AVOID
ABDICATING CONTROL

Keep Personal Boundaries Intact

Valerie sat in traffic and mulled over the events of the day. As she tapped her brakes in rhythm with the car in front of her, she reviewed the incident. Could she have done something differently? Could she have done something better?

A new business associate, Tom, had relocated to her office a couple of months ago. The first few weeks she hardly saw him. She was busy with the Anderson project, and he was busy learning the ropes of a new system. They'd run across each other in the halls, but frankly, she'd been too busy to do more than look up from her paperwork and nod her head in greeting.

About a week ago Tom had come to her desk unannounced. She'd been surprised to look up and see him there. She got the vague impression he'd been looking at her for a while. Deciding she had a few minutes to spare, and out of politeness to a new coworker, she asked how the job was going, if he'd found a place to stay, if he was getting settled. He perched on the edge of her desk, swinging his leg off to the side. She thought it was odd he'd passed up the padded chair in front of the desk. The odd feeling persisted throughout the conversation, which she carefully tried to keep neutral. It was his final remark about the improvement in "the scenery" that started bells going off in her head.

But the look he'd given her was ambivalent, and she couldn't pin down anything concrete in their conversation. She had her suspicions, but she gave him the benefit of the doubt. Her husband agreed it was probably nothing, but she promised to be alert during any future encounters with Tom.

The "future" ended up being that afternoon. The conversation started with Tom's verbal appreciation of her outfit. He especially liked how her jacket accentuated her figure, which he said was great for a woman her age. Tom looked her up and down and said it was obvious she still kept herself in great shape. She didn't know what part bothered her more, the figure part or the age part. Whichever it was, Valerie came to a quick conclusion. She'd had enough.

Instead of thanking Tom for the compliment, she walked around the front of the desk, facing him squarely. Calmly, she explained she preferred to keep business relationships based on professional conversations. He looked perplexed and asked her if she didn't want to be friends with the people she worked with. After all, he said, he was just trying to be friendly.

Valerie repeated her statement again, verbatim. Tom wondered aloud what he'd said that offended her. Again, she repeated her preference—no apology, no explanation. She thanked him for coming by and wished him well at the new job. She made it quite clear the conversation was over for that day.

Stuck in the gridlock of after-work traffic, Valerie was clear on something else. Tom had pushed up against her personal boundaries, and they had held.

CUTTING DOWN ON THE CONFUSION

How many times do you suppose innocent Joseph sat in his cell and asked himself if he had inadvertently done or said something to give wrong signals to his master's dangerous wife? It's so easy to begin to second guess your actions when confronted with a sexually charged encounter. Was there something you said to lead the person on? Did you yourself misunderstand the signals the other person was sending out? Did you make an incorrect assumption? Are you making too much out of it?

Add to that the guilt that can be present if you've previously engaged in inappropriate speech with the other person because you didn't want to seem prudish. Or the embarrassment of realizing someone you didn't suspect was thinking about you in a sexual way.

Amid all of these unpleasant feelings, the tendency for many people is to shove the whole thing into the back of their minds where it's easier to ignore. Pretend it didn't happen. Hope it will just go away. This, of course, just contributes to the confusion.

Matters are further complicated by the changing rules of male-female interaction. As the pendulum swings from one extreme to the next, the question becomes, "Where are we in the path of the blade?" We have swung away from the extreme of men being able to harass women with impunity. Some men still view women as merely sexual objects, but procedures and policies are now in place to support women who resist inappropriate pressure. But the pendulum blade has begun to arc in the opposite direction.

Granted, some men in the past have used their position in business to gain control over female coworkers. Now some women are beginning to use their positions as weapons of control. Potiphar's wife wasn't the only woman whose indecent demands have ruined a good man. Women in positions of power have been accused by subordinate men of sexual harassment. Women in subordinate positions have unfairly accused men in prestigious corporate positions of inappropriate conduct, hoping to gain control over their bosses or their work situation.

Whichever position is being exploited, power or subordination, control is really the key element. Sex is just the most prominent component.

MAINTAINING SELF-CONTROL WITH A SUPERIOR

Most of us, if we don't totally love our jobs, at least need them. We have mortgages or rent. We have cars to pay off and braces to finance. We have vacation plans and hopes for retirement. Our lives often revolve around our jobs, with established family schedules and routines in place to accommodate our work. To leave our jobs would be difficult. Supervisors or superiors at work who have the ability to affect our jobs therefore wield power in our lives. Some will attempt to use that power to their personal sexual advantage.

No job, no amount of money, no promise of reward is worth trading in your self-esteem, your self-control. Depending on who is pressuring you, you may need to fight to keep control over your own life and your own sexuality. It may help you to know you are not powerless. Consider some steps you can take to keep control of your life. We do not presume to offer you legal advice on such matters, but a bit of wisdom and some common sense can see you safely through most sticky moments in the workplace. If all else fails, run like Joseph did.

Control How You Are Spoken To

Do not allow your supervisor to speak to you disrespectfully. Just because someone is above you in the organizational structure of the company, they do not have the right to verbally minimize you. It is important to voice an objection to this behavior as it occurs. Putting it off until later removes the immediacy of both their actions and your feelings about that action. For example, if a supervisor speaks to you using vulgar language or launches into criticism laced with personal references, you need to object.

"Mr. Smith, I would appreciate it if you would please refrain from using vulgar language when you speak to me."

"Ms. Jones, if you have a complaint about my work product, I naturally am concerned about that, but I cannot allow you to continue to speak to me in this way."

Speaking to a subordinate in an attacking or demeaning manner is one way a sexual manipulator will attempt to gain acquiescence from a target. If they find out you will not stand up for yourself in a verbal assault, chances are they will expect the same capitulation in a sexual confrontation. Often, a sexual manipulator will size up a potential target in this way. By voicing a timely and firm objection, it may be possible to forestall sexual aggression early in the process.

If your supervisor is making inappropriate personal comments, the simplest thing to do is to ask them to stop. Be firm but professional. Make your objections every time inappropriate comments are made. Do not wait. Put bosses on notice that you do not appreciate comments of that nature and fully expect comments like that to cease. If the comments do not stop, write a memorandum to the supervisor and send a copy to your human relations or personnel office, outlining in detail the nature of the offensive comments and your repeated requests for them to cease. If it should become necessary for you to contemplate legal action, documentation of your perception of the events written down at the time they occurred will be invaluable.

Control the Situation by Bringing in Reinforcements

The personnel director looked over her papers, incredulous. She couldn't believe what she was hearing and seeing. Part of her didn't want to believe it. Mr. Jackson was one of the sharpest buyers in the firm. Now he was being accused by one of his assistants of repeated incidents of sexual harassment. They weren't going to be happy about this upstairs. No, not at all.

But Sally had put together an impressive report of each incident: what she'd said, what he'd said, what had happened from her point of view. Her complaint was impossible to ignore. As a woman, she knew she shouldn't ignore it. As the personnel director, she knew she couldn't ignore it. She was required both by law and by company policy to investigate and recommend appropriate action.

Sally was looking to her to help, to do the right thing. She really had no choice, no matter how much flak was about to explode in the skies around her. As bad as it was going to be for her, it was going to be twice as hard for Sally. Good thing she'd documented everything. When the company lawyers started asking their questions, the offenses would be down on paper and not just a series of her later recollections.

Taking a deep breath, she thanked Sally for bringing the incidents to her attention. Reaching into her file, she pulled out a company policy sheet explaining what would happen next in the process. Sally looked over everything carefully, composure intact. She didn't look happy, just resolved.

Since supervisors who are sexual manipulators know they hold power over a person's livelihood, the threats they employ to force sexual compliance from a target can be veiled. They don't need to boldly threaten a job. The employee is very much aware of that person's influence over job reviews, employee evaluations, promotions, and even hiring and firing. In the shock of a sexual ultimatum tied to your job, your first reaction may be to think you completely mis-understood. You have only one way to know—ask. Depending on how bold your supervisor is, they may counter with another euphemism for sexual compliance. Fight euphemism with clarity. If you are convinced the boss intends sexual pressure, file a complaint, either through your own office or through the Equal Employment Opportunity Commission (EEOC) of the federal government. Sexual pressure placed on a subordinate by a superior is against the law.

If you are touched improperly or assaulted in a sexual way by a supervisor, report the incident immediately. Serious, blatant assaults should be reported to the authorities. Although you may experience pressure to "keep it within the company," your supervisor has committed a crime against you. As a citizen of this country, you are entitled to personal protection from all sexual assaults, including those by supervisors.

Remember, one of the messages you must get across clearly to the offender is your complete disapproval of and discomfort with their speech and/or actions. If you are not clear in your protests, a supervisor could claim you participated in the conversation or activity without objection.

Avoid Over-Friendly Skies

In some work relationships, traveling with opposite-sex associates may by necessary. If you are a subordinate scheduled to take a business trip with a superior, here are a few things to remember.

1. *The purpose of a business trip is business.* Whatever the location of the trip, the purpose is still to conduct business. Hawaii may be the resort destination for 99.9 percent of the people on the airplane, but if you're going there for business, don't be swayed by paradise.

2. *Know your responsibilities ahead of time.* Ask beforehand about the goals and schedule for the business trip. Be aware before you leave of what you'll be doing each day and what the business-related

expectations are. Doing this will allow you to better prepare for your responsibilities regarding the trip. It will also alert you if your supervisor has other, sexualized, reasons for wanting you to come along.

3. Keep control over your personal time and space. A business trip may require you to be away from home for twenty-four, forty-eight, or more hours, but this doesn't mean that all of those hours become the exclusive property of your superior. You should not be required to eat all meals with your traveling partner. You should never be required to entertain your opposite-sex traveling partner in your room, nor should you be required to conduct business in theirs. Often hotels will have work areas you can use, or they have no problem with you setting up an informal meeting in a corner of the hotel lobby.

4. Avoid loosening your personal standards because of an unfamiliar environment. Sometimes, when we are far from home, we are tempted to "loosen up." If you would not allow certain behavior or speech from someone while at work, do not allow it merely because it is occurring away from the office. If you would not allow certain behavior or speech from yourself while at work, do not allow yourself to engage in it merely because you are doing it away from the office.

5. Stay connected to family. If you are married, take a picture of your family with you. Whenever possible, call your family each night when you get back to your room. Because you may be hundreds or thousands of miles away from your family, remain connected to them by thinking about them, praying about them, talking about them. Remind whoever you are traveling with, and yourself, of the other relationships in your life.

6. Be wise whenever you and your traveling partner have to be alone together. Maintain your professional demeanor. You may not be as high up in the company as they are, but you are still a professional.

Acting like one continually reinforces the message that to you this excursion is for business only.

MAINTAINING SELF-CONTROL
WITH A SUBORDINATE

Many people find power to be an aphrodisiac. They are drawn to it. They want to be part of it. If they cannot earn power or gain it through the course of their own efforts, they may attempt to co-opt power from an influential person through initiating a sexual relationship with that individual. These people are the sexual climbers outlined in the previous chapter.

Whereas the sexual manipulator is looking to control a sexual relationship for the sex, the sexual climber is looking to control a sexual relationship for the relationship and the perks that go with it. Through the relationship with a superior the sexual climber obtains special favors in exchange for sexual performance. The favors could be a biased job evaluation, personal notoriety, professional advancement or career help.

Remember, a sexual climber is interested in the tangible benefits of a relationship. Sex is, therefore, just one way to solidify a relationship with a powerful individual. If the targeted superior is susceptible to seduction, the sexual climber will use that method fairly quickly. If the person is not susceptible to sex initially, the sexual climber will hold off sexual pressure until they are reasonably sure the pressure will work. In the interim the sexual climber will use other methods to bond with the target, such as offering an exemplary, overly dedicated work product. But how do you know if a person is just a great employee or a sexual climber? Eventually, the sexual climber will move the focus of the relationship from work areas to personal areas. In so many words they will eventually attempt to introduce a sexual component into the working relationship.

As the person in control of most aspects of a professional relationship, a supervisor can take steps to minimize the effectiveness of a sexual climber. The most important, obviously, is to keep yourself morally pure. If you refuse to make yourself vulnerable sexually to the temptations of a sexual climber, the climber will eventually move on to greener pastures and target someone else.

Be wise in how you deal with subordinates.

1. Avoid private, secluded meetings. Try, as much as possible, to let other people know when and where you will be meeting subordinates and for what reason.

2. Whenever possible, keep the door to your office open or ajar. Purposely choose to keep your voice lowered to minimize the chances of someone overhearing business you are talking about. Most discussions are work-related anyway. Other people are busy with their own work and too preoccupied to spend precious time trying to listen in on your conversations.

3. Whenever possible, include other people in your meetings. Not only will you cut down on the number of meetings, but you'll protect yourself against either unfounded charges or unwelcome advances by a subordinate.

4. Avoid after-hours, solitary meetings with a subordinate of the opposite sex. Conduct business during business hours. If you're too busy to get to it today, leave it for tomorrow. You really should be home with your family anyway.

5. Make arrangements to have a witness. If you suspect a subordinate of being a sexual climber and find it necessary to conduct a personnel review or other meeting that needs to be private, instruct a secretary or coworker to make a prearranged entrance into your office. Later, if a problem arises, you will have a witness to the demeanor during the meeting in question.

Sound like a lot of hassle? You're right, it is. But it's nothing compared to the disruption of your life and career if you are targeted by a sexual climber or accused unjustly of a sexual overture. Honest coworkers and subordinates will appreciate your discretion, the maintenance of your personal integrity, and the care you extend toward them.

MAINTAINING SELF-CONTROL AND SEXUAL INTEGRITY

Whether you are in a supervisory or subordinate role, God expects you to maintain sexual integrity. If you are being pressured by a supervisor to have sex, do not give in. Never compromise your values, your morals, or your faith because your job is threatened. Trust God to protect you and to be with you as you confront your sexual manipulator. Trust God to take care of you if you determine it is best for you to leave your job. If God expects you to symbolically cut off a hand or gouge out an eye so as not to sin (Matthew 5:29–30), trust him to sustain you if you have to give up a paycheck to keep yourself sexually pure.

If you are being propositioned by a subordinate for sex, do not give in to temptation. Why risk the eternal riches of heaven for the temporary rush of a sexual encounter? Remember the verse from Proverbs quoted earlier about a prostitute reducing you to a loaf of bread? (6:26). The sexual climber has reduced you to a favorable job rating, a slot on a social calendar, or a doctored job evaluation. Why sell yourself for such a paltry price when your very life, your sexuality included, has already been bought and paid for through the priceless blood of Jesus?

In all of your business dealings, especially those involving a disparity in position, you must work to keep yourself above reproach. (This is true, not just in business settings. Subsequent chapters will deal specifically with counseling and pastoral situations.)

BE PROACTIVE—PROJECT RESPECT

Do you realize that the way other people treat you may be shaped by the way you feel about and treat yourself? You can set the tone for most of your relationships. Conducting yourself in an aboveboard manner shows that you respect yourself and others. So keep your personal standards high. "Be careful to do what is right in the eyes of everybody" (Romans 12:17).

1. Do not allow obscenities to be used in your presence. This can be difficult in certain work situations, but it is important. Most businesses have employee handbooks that outline proper and improper employee behavior, encompassing all employees of the company. The use of obscenities either between coworkers or between employees and customers is generally frowned upon. Obscenities are unprofessional, and most businesses spend a good deal of time and effort to enhance their professionalism. Exceptions do exist, of course. That is where your own personal boundaries come in. You may not be able to squelch every curse word spoken within a one-hundred-yard radius, but you can insist that obscenities not be used by someone speaking directly to you. This personal boundary should be stated calmly, clearly, and consistently. Repeat it as many times as it takes to get your point across. Since many obscenities contain a sexual component, disallowing obscenities will remove some sexual speech.

2. Do not participate in sexual or crude jokes. By listening to them without protest, you give approval. By telling them without restraint, you broadcast your willingness to engage in sexual matters. By participating in them without restriction, you encourage the introduction of lust into your work situation. Some may take your participation with them in sexual or crude speech as an invitation to explore other sexual avenues with you.

3. Do not underestimate the power of lust. Its potential is present whenever a sexual component is added to a situation. By failing to protest or by contributing to sexually charged speech or jokes, you broadcast your sexuality. You broadcast your willingness to be viewed by others through the lens of sexuality. For some of those around you, if not yourself, this gives lust the foothold it needs to break down the door of personal boundaries. Once lust has gained entrance into a situation, the impact of its power is difficult for many people to contain. Lust is one genie you want to keep bottled up, especially at work.

4. Discourage personal, revelatory conversations with members of the opposite sex. The deeper the conversations, the more chance the content will eventually become sexual. If, during the course of your job, you deem it necessary to speak to someone about deeply personal matters, make sure a third party is present. The third party should be someone you trust, a sensible friend, who can act as a buffer for the conversation. Explain that because of the highly personal nature of the conversation you feel compelled to have, you have invited this other person to be present for everybody's protection.

5. Object immediately if someone else touches you in an inappropriate way. The time to object to a sexual touch or caress is when it happens. Too often, in the utter surprise of the moment, the tendency is to explain it away or deny it. While you are busy second-guessing whether it really happened, the other person will be busy figuring out how to do it again.

But how do you know if the touch was intentional or accidental? In the busy crush of an office or the hampered space of a copy room, people will accidentally touch each other. In most cases, one or both of the parties involved with accidental touching will automatically become embarrassed and apologize. But accidentally touching someone inappropriately is a rare occurrence. If it's happening on a regular basis with the same person, chances are it's not accidental. Once you've determined a pattern to the "accidental" touching, object to it the very next time it happens. Put the incident in writing, if necessary. Be quite clear that touching of this kind will not be permitted by you in any circumstance.

The bottom line in all of this is to maintain your self-control—your control over your self, your body, your person—in work situations. No matter who you are working for, you need to guard your personal integrity. This holds true twenty-four hours a day, seven days a week, fifty-two weeks a year. God does not compartmentalize your life. He is just as concerned with your conduct at work on Monday as he is with your conduct at church on Sunday. Even when a manipulator beckoned him to her bed, Joseph knew he was God's man, and he said so!

—————— Fuel for Thought ——————

God is aware that sexual manipulators and climbers exist. He knows they will tempt you to sin against him, against yourself, against your family. He also prepares a way of escape for you in every temptation so that you will be able to bear it (1 Corinthians 10:13).

Remember also, your actions are viewed by others and compared with what you say about yourself. Others will look at your actions as a Christian, and make judgments about God and Christ. As an ambassador for Christ, you have a responsibility in every work situation to present your allegiance to your Master in the best possible light. You are a light, a light on a hill. Your actions shine for all to see. So be wise in how you conduct yourself as you do business.

1. Look over the following passages from Proverbs and relate them to conduct at work. In your notebook or binder, write what each passage might be saying to help you with either a sexual manipulator or a sexual climber. What might each

passage be saying to you if you are yourself engaging in patterns of sexual manipulation or sexual climbing?

> The man of integrity walks securely, but he who takes crooked paths will be found out. (Proverbs 10:9)

> The righteousness of the upright delivers them, but the unfaithful are trapped by evil desires. (Proverbs 11:6)

> Like a gold ring in a pig's snout is a beautiful woman who shows no discretion. (Proverbs 11:22)

> An evil man is trapped by his sinful talk, but a righteous man escapes trouble. (Proverbs 12:13)

> A righteous man is cautious in friendship, but the way of the wicked leads them astray. (Proverbs 12:26)

> A wise man's heart guides his mouth, and his lips promote instruction. (Proverbs 16:23)

> He who winks with his eye is plotting perversity; he who purses his lips is bent on evil. (Proverbs 16:30)

> A fool's mouth is his undoing, and his lips are a snare to his soul. (Proverbs 18:7)

> Food gained by fraud tastes sweet to a man, but he ends up with a mouth full of gravel. (Proverbs 20:17)

> Like a muddied spring or a polluted well is a righteous man who gives way to the wicked. (Proverbs 25:26)

2. Now that you have read over these verses, write down anything God was specifically telling you personally.

3. List three characteristics of Joseph that allowed him to flee from Potiphar's wife. Considering these characteristics, do you think Joseph would have done anything differently if he knew he would still end up in prison? What does this say about what Joseph considered valuable?

MAY GOD GRANT YOU CLEAR VISION *to see the way of escape he has prepared in work-related temptations. May he grant you protection from the schemes of evil people who plot to use you for their selfish purposes. May he bolster your efforts to maintain your sexual integrity as a beacon to others of your trust in him.*

PEOPLE POLLUTE
EVEN GOD'S
BEAUTIFUL CREATION
OF FAMILY.

7

RECOGNIZE
THE POWER OF FAMILY TIES

Love within the Family
Can Be Devastating

The bench outside the courtroom was cold
and hard. The heart inside the man who sat
on the bench was the same. It had been warm and soft, once. No
longer, hardened as it was by years of despicable conduct and ridiculous denials, mostly to himself. He sat outside the courtroom, ready
to deny it one more time. Ready to look his girls in the face and say
to anyone who would listen that they were lying; that he was telling
the truth.

After all, he thought to himself as he squirmed on the bench, he
was their father. This was about his family—about his right to make
rules for the family as he saw fit. They were his daughters. It wasn't
anybody else's business what went on inside his house. This was private. He shouldn't have to justify himself to anyone. He shouldn't
have to explain himself to anyone. Wasn't any of their business.

Agitated, he stood up. Down the hall he saw one of the lawyers
peek her head out of a doorway. The rest of the family would be in
there, he guessed, staying as far away from him as they could. Like

they didn't want to be seen with him. Like they weren't part of the same family even.

The girls he could understand. Their minds had been swayed by that social worker at school. It was Betty he couldn't figure. Why, it wasn't like she hadn't known what was going on. Wasn't like she hadn't stayed with him through all of it, never saying a word. Why, it was as much her fault as it was his. And it wasn't even his fault. It was the girls' fault, really. They never should have said anything about it to anybody. It was family business and nobody else's.

Stanley spat into the cigarette sand nearby and sat back down again on the uncomfortable bench. It didn't fit him, and he was disgusted with the whole business. He couldn't wait until it was over and done with and he could get back to work. The whole thing had happened years ago anyway. Why'd they have to go and bring it up again?

Home. A word that is supposed to bring up images of security and love. Images of a place where you can relax and be yourself. Where you are loved and accepted for who you are. Where each member of the family feels safe when the front door closes, locking out an often hectic, stress-filled world.

Family. A word that is supposed to bring up images of continuity and belonging. A close-knit group where each member has a defined role. Where children can just be kids, growing up in a nurturing, loving environment with adults who are dedicated to their total well-being. In a turbulent world where relationships shift and change, the relationships of family are supposed to be the steady core that stabilizes our sense of self.

Home. Family. Supposed to be. But supposed to be doesn't always happen. For some the home is not a place of refuge with the front door shut to keep evil out. Instead, for too many home is a place of lurking danger with the front door shut to keep evil secret. For them family is not an environment offering love and support.

Instead, it is a place of perverted relationships where sick, twisted love is demanded.

SEXUALIZED RELATIONSHIPS WITHIN THE IMMEDIATE FAMILY

Husband and wife. Father and daughter. Mother and son. Brother and sister. These are special relationships born of family ties. Within them lies knowledge and history, understanding and commitment. Within them only one should be sexualized—husband and wife. Unfortunately, this is not the case in all families.

When family members other than husband and wife seek sexual gratification from each other, the only possible outcome is destruction and devastation for all those involved. The very core of trust so essential to a family is shattered by the sexual perversion we call incest.

Nature versus Nurture

No one is required to take a test to determine if they are emotionally or psychologically ready to become a parent. The only criteria is physical ability to procreate. For some people the ability to produce a child outpaces their emotional ability to raise it. Instead of being the focal point of what the parent can give, the child becomes the provider of what the parent needs.

Young children are predisposed to love and trust their parents, to look to them to fill their needs, from the most basic needs when we are young to the more complex ones as we grow and mature. So in our tender years we are the most vulnerable of victims if an adult who is our parent turns out to be a sexual predator. In such cases, where parents seek sexual gratification from their offspring, nature gets turned on its head. The ones whose needs should be supplied by a parent wind up supplying the out-of-control needs of that parent.

Some men need sexual gratification through perversion.

Depending on the depth of their depravity, they sexualize their relationship with their child, usually a daughter, even while the child is an infant or a toddler. Others will wait until the child is older but not yet to puberty to begin their pattern of sexual abuse.

As the child and her ability to reason and respond develops, the father's sexual abuse may end or take on a different form. Having been groomed by the misbehaving parent to respond within this sexualized relationship, the child may seem to become more of a willing participant than a coerced victim. This acquiescence on the part of the child may be used by the parent as justification to continue the abuse. But the guilt the child feels about "allowing" the abuse, or in some cases even gaining physical gratification from the abuse, can be devastating.

This sin is not sexist. Mothers can also have perverted needs. Some women crave sexual control through companionship. Their ability to control all aspects of their child's life, including the child's body, gives them a sense of satisfaction that can translate into a sexual thing. What begins as maternal devotion and control over nourishing and caring for the child, usually a son, can become sexualized possession of that child. As the son grows and matures, the mother's physical connection to the child may contain increasingly sexualized elements of inappropriate touching and arousal. The child is not viewed as a distinct person in his own right in such cases but as an extension of the mother's need. In order to maintain her control over her child, the mother may use increasingly sexualized means to exploit or warp her son's own emerging sexuality in order to further bond him to herself.

In either of these cases, the sexualized nature of the parent-child relationship causes extensive and often long-lasting damage. For the children caught in this sexual prison, childhood is a nightmare of sexual ambush in which they are called upon to fulfill adult desires they only vaguely comprehend. Violence, fear, and guilt fill their youthful days. For the adult children who emerge from this kind of a childhood, adulthood is often a nightmare of anguished memories and immense difficulty in establishing and maintaining healthy adult relationships.

Brotherly Love

Pamela hung up the phone in disgust. Somehow he'd found her again. Wearily she picked up the receiver to contact the telephone company. How many numbers, all unlisted, had she gone through in the past five years? She'd quit keeping count. It almost wasn't worth having friends, always having to tell them her number was being changed. All because her brother refused to leave her alone.

But that had always been his problem. He'd started molesting her when she was five and he was nine. It had started with him wanting her to touch him and continued with him wanting to touch her as they got older.

It had been their little secret, just the two of them. She had so desperately wanted the love and affection of her older brother. She hadn't realized at first there was anything wrong with how he wanted to show her that love and affection. At least he noticed her and played with her, as long as she would "play" with him later when they were alone.

Eventually, of course, she came to know that what they were doing was wrong and that he was wrong to have wanted her to do those things in the first place. By then, he was not just older; he was bigger and stronger. He threatened to tell their parents, her friends, her boyfriends. She was caught in a terrible trap of wanting to get away but not wanting to risk exposure and humiliation. So she began to find ways to avoid him whenever she could. When she was fourteen, he moved out of the house into an apartment with some friends from school. That was the happiest day of her life.

After that Pamela became almost phobic about her brother's visits home. She could come up with an instant excuse about why she either needed to be somewhere else or why she just had to spend the night at a friend's house. Her parents never seemed to track her reluctance to be under the same roof as her brother. To them she was just a busy teen who didn't have time for any of the family.

For several years, she didn't hear from him at all. Then, after she'd been out of her parent's house for almost a year, she began to get strange phone calls. Just breathing or silence on the other end. Somehow she knew it was him. Angry, she shouted during one such call that she knew who he was. He admitted it and began to reminisce about their time growing up together. He talked about coming over to her apartment soon, just to "talk about old times."

The next week she moved, got a post office box for her mail, and got her first unlisted phone number. Finally in desperation she told her parents what had happened during her childhood, begging them not to give out any information about her. They didn't believe her. Took his side in everything. After that she broke off contact with all of them.

The woman on the other end of the line was professional and efficient. She would give Pamela a new number within a few days and, yes, it would be unlisted. She reminded Pamela to be careful about giving out her new number.

If only it were that simple, Pamela thought.

In addition to parent-child relationships becoming sexualized within a family, sibling relationships may also turn sexual. The danger of this happening increases if an inappropriately sexualized relationship already exists within the family. If, for example, the father has sex with his daughter, any sons may pattern their behavior after their father. Thus the daughter becomes a sexualized target for all the males in the house.

But sexualized sibling relationships can occur without parental incest to trigger them. Generally, sibling sex occurs when one of the children approaches adolescence and inappropriately uses another for sexual exploration. Case studies show that the target is almost always younger. While the initial reason for the sexual contact with younger children is exploration rather than gratification, this can change as age increases and a response of sexual gratification becomes physically possible.

For older children, of course, gratification is a goal, as well as the control inherent in dominating another person sexually. For the corollaries to sexual abuse almost always are control and utter self-absorption. The aggressor within any of these sexualized relationships is using sex as a way to control the victim. Their need for ironclad control stems from their complete focus on their own desires. Sexual aggressors within the family sexualize these relationships because they are convenient. Their victims are literally right at hand and, because of the family ties, are already subject to a certain level of control. While they may seek to molest others outside the family, often they do not need to leave the front yard to search for sexual targets.

SEXUALIZED RELATIONSHIPS
WITHIN THE EXTENDED FAMILY

Is there anything better than a family reunion to bring everybody together? Moms, dads, sisters, brothers, aunts, uncles, nieces, nephews, cousins—all the clan. Extended family. Sometimes people you've never met or seldom seen. All ages. A web of relationships woven together. Sometimes, the fabric of those relationships can fray.

For people predisposed to sexualizing relationships, the extended family can provide fertile ground. They may feel constrained not to target immediate family but have no problem sighting members of their extended family. They take advantage of both the closeness of the family and the distance of extended relationships to choose targets for sexualization.

Again, it is a question of convenience. Because everyone is "family," plenty of hugs and kisses are going around. This closeness gives the sexual manipulator the cover to probe for potential targets. A kiss on the mouth instead of the cheek. A hand rubbing up and down a back instead of a hand on the arm. A caress of the buttocks instead of a pat on the back. A hungry look accompanying a comment about how someone looks or how much they've grown or how big they've gotten.

The distance of the extended family can bring about a false sense of otherness. People who would never choose a child or sibling may target a niece or nephew, a grandchild or cousin. Kissing cousins aren't always what they seem to be. Sexual boundaries that hold firm with strangers somehow sag for some when extended family comes to town.

SEXUALIZED RELATIONSHIPS WITHIN A BLENDED FAMILY

The closeness of family ties has often been used to pervert family relationships. In some homes normal prohibitions against this kind of behavior simply are missing. Add to this moral vacuum the fact that the *Leave It to Beaver* version of the American family has radically shifted over the years. Now more and more people flow in and out of the family unit. With so many strangers living in the same house, the potential for sexualized relationships within blended families must be recognized.

Jill was ten years old when her mother married Ted. Her real father had left when she was almost six. She had heard from him a couple of times, but he'd married again within two years and now had a new family in a different state. Her mother had dated a couple of other guys before marrying Ted.

She'd come to Jill and asked her what she thought of Ted. Said she was thinking about marrying him. Jill had told her mom it really didn't matter to her. What she hadn't said was the reason it didn't matter. What did matter to Jill wasn't going to happen. Before her dad had remarried, getting her mom and dad back together was all that mattered to Jill. Now that wasn't possible, so Jill had kind of turned herself off about who her mother dated. And Ted seemed nice enough. He brought her a toy or candy every time he came to pick up her mom. Sometimes, she was even allowed to go with them to a ball game or a movie. Jill could tell her mom really wanted her to be okay with it. So she said she was.

Now she wasn't okay with it, but she didn't know how to tell her mother. At first, Ted was fine. He pretty much left the parenting up to Jill's mom and only got really mad at her once in a while. As long as she was quiet, stayed out of his way, and didn't take up too much of her mom's time, Ted was no problem.

Lately, though, it was getting harder to stay out of Ted's way. He always seemed to find her, wherever she was. Always asking about her boyfriends and what they did. He kept making comments about how her body was changing and what a beautiful young woman she was becoming. Young woman—and she wasn't even fourteen yet. It made her feel creepy when he'd look at her longer than she thought he should. Before he had never seemed to mind if he didn't see her all day. Now he was making it a habit to come into her room to say good night before she went to bed. He'd never really been that affectionate before. Now he gave her a kiss every time he saw her. And Mom acted like everything was okay.

As marriages break up and families scatter, many people find themselves plunged into new relationships. Parents remarry, merging family units and bringing together people who have no blood ties to each other. Within this fluidity some will inevitably sexualize their new relationships.

As we've said before, to a person who inappropriately sexualizes relationships, the family is fertile ground. This problem is compounded when the family is blended and traditional prohibitions against sexualized relationships between family members are weakened. Because the children of one spouse are not related by blood to the other spouse, members of a blended family may be viewed as potential sexual partners.

No one would condone a man's leaving his wife and marrying his daughter. However, the lines are not quite so clear when a man leaves his wife and marries one of his wife's adopted daughters. Remember the actor and film director Woody Allen, his actress wife, Mia Farrow, and her adopted daughter, Soon Ye Previn? Soon Ye became Mia Farrow's adopted daughter when Mia Farrow was married to music conductor Andre Previn. When Mia Farrow subsequently married Woody Allen, she brought along her children from the previous marriage. After a number of years, her marriage to Woody Allen also began to dissolve. Controversy erupted when the media revealed that Woody Allen was sexually involved with Soon Ye, by now a young adult. After his divorce from Mia Farrow, Woody Allen married stepdaughter Soon Ye. Woody Allen evidently saw nothing wrong with his sexual relationship with his daughter by marriage. Mia Farrow found everything wrong with it, publicly admitting feelings of outrage and betrayal.

While this case was highly publicized, it is by no means unique in our world. Daytime talk shows have made convoluted sexualized relationships of this type fodder for ratings. Sometimes the sidebar explaining the relationship of the person shown on the screen is three lines long: "Daughter from mother's first marriage having sex with second husband's brother."

Tragically, the blended families of today often become the broken marriages of tomorrow. Studies consistently show second and subsequent marriages failing at higher rates than first ones. This instability further degrades the boundaries against intrafamily sexual relationships. At some point Woody Allen no longer looked at Soon Ye as his stepdaughter. Perhaps the shift took place around the time he began to distance himself from her mother, Mia Farrow. With wobbly sexual barriers at best, the shake-up of the current family can cause them to teeter and topple.

HOPE FOR THOSE WHO HAVE STRAYED

Far too many people enter their adulthood burdened with the pain, guilt, and shame of an inappropriately sexualized family relationship. God never intended for the family to be perverted in this way. But people, with their sinful nature, have found a way to pollute even God's beautiful creation of family.

If you are one of those who have wounded members of your family—immediate, extended, or blended—by bringing sex into relationships where it does not belong, you are not without hope for redemption. It is true, God has seen every vile thing you have done. It is true, he has wept for your sins. It is true, also, he has died for them. You cannot go back and undo the damage you have done to others and to yourself, but you can gain forgiveness and healing. Though the ones you have hurt may not be able to forgive you, God is able. If you are truly penitent in heart and behavior, God is able to forgive you.

If you have a history of sexually abusing someone in your family, look over the following signs of sexual addiction and honestly evaluate them in regard to your own actions, thoughts, and feelings (from *Don't Call It Love: Recovery from Sexual Addiction* by Patrick Carnes).

1. A pattern of out-of-control behavior.

2. Severe consequences due to sexual behavior.

3. Inability to stop despite adverse consequences.

4. Persistent pursuit of self-destructive or high-risk behavior.

5. Ongoing desire or effort to limit sexual behavior.

6. Sexual obsession and fantasy as a primary coping strategy.

7. Increasing amounts of sexual experience because the current level of activity is no longer sufficient.

6. Severe mood changes around sexual activity.

9. Inordinate amounts of time spent in obtaining sex, being sexual, or recovering from sexual experience.

10. Neglect of important social, occupational, or recreational activities because of sexual behavior.

If you can identify with these ten points, you need to seek professional help in coming to terms with possible sexual addiction. You owe it to your family and to yourself to get the help you need to overcome this sexual obsession.

If you are one of the multitude who have been sexually wounded within the family, who feel isolated and alone in your past, God is with you now. He was with you then. He was there during every moment of your shame and hurt. He felt every tear that traced a track down your cheek. He has wept himself for the sins committed against you.

You may not have had a choice about the type of family you grew up in, but you have a choice now. God's invitation to become his child is always available to you. In him you can find the perfect Father, the perfect Parent. In Jesus you can find the caring Brother. With God's help you can reconstruct a healthy loving family, full of children, mothers and fathers, brothers and sisters, grandparents and grandchildren. God and his family wait for you to join with them and to experience the healing of his Spirit.

─────── Fuel for Thought ───────

1. Think back over your past family relationships. If they were free from inappropriate sexualization, take a moment and thank God.

2. If some family relationships were painful to you, write down the source of the pain in your notebook or binder. Indicate where you are in the process of admitting your own responsibility in that pain, if appropriate. Indicate, also, where you are in the process of forgiving those involved, including yourself.

3. Is there someone you need to communicate with? Either to admit guilt and seek forgiveness or to communicate the pain you are feeling regarding their actions toward you? Compose a letter to them. (It is not necessary for you to mail the letter at this time. It may be enough just for you to articulate your thoughts.)

4. Spend some time in prayer to God. Give him praise for the gift of Jesus. Thank him for his love and his plan for you to be called his child. Pour out to him your heart.

5. Listen to what God tells you and be obedient to his voice.

Helpful Resource: Patrick Carnes's book *Don't Call It Love: Recovery from Sexual Addiction* is "must" reading for anybody who has sexually abused a family member or for anyone who has suffered such mistreatment. He helps us place blame where blame belongs.

MAY GOD BLESS YOU AS YOU PUT *your past into perspective. May his Spirit provide you comfort and healing. May God grant you courage to repair any relationships you have damaged. May the promise of his forgiveness give you hope.*

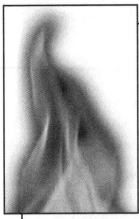

AMNON SON OF DAVID FELL IN LOVE WITH TAMAR, the beautiful sister of Absalom son of David.

Now Amnon had a friend named Jonadab son of Shimeah, David's brother. He asked Amnon, "Why do you look so haggard morning after morning?"

"I'm in love with Tamar, my brother Absalom's sister."

"Go to bed and pretend to be ill," Jonadab said. "When your father comes to see you, say to him, 'I would like my sister Tamar to come and give me something to eat.'"

David sent word to Tamar at the palace. Tamar went to the house of her brother Amnon. She made the bread in his sight. Then she took the pan and served him the bread, but he refused to eat.

Amnon said to Tamar, "Bring the food here into my bedroom so that I may eat from your hand." But when she took it to him to eat, he grabbed her and said, "Come to bed with me, my sister."

"Don't, my brother! Don't do this wicked thing. Please speak to the king; he will not keep me from being married to you." But he refused to listen to her, and he raped her.

Then Amnon hated her and said to her, "Get up and get out!"

Tamar put ashes on her head and tore the ornamented robe she was wearing. She went away, weeping aloud as she went.

Her brother Absalom said to her, "Has that Amnon, your brother, been with you? Be quiet now, my sister; he is your brother. Don't take this thing to heart." And Tamar lived in her brother Absalom's house, a desolate woman.

When King David heard all this, he was furious. Absalom never said a word to Amnon; he hated Amnon because he had disgraced his sister Tamar.

Two years later, when Absalom's sheep-shearers were at Baal Hazor, he invited all the king's sons to come there.

"No, my son," the king replied. "All of us should not go; we would only be a burden to you."

Then Absalom said, "If not, please let my brother Amnon come with us."

Absalom ordered his men, "Listen! When Amnon is in high spirits from drinking wine and I say to you, 'Strike Amnon down,' then kill him." Absalom's men did to Amnon what Absalom had ordered.

King David mourned for his son every day.

—from 2 Samuel 13

8

The path of the righteous is like the first gleam of dawn, shining ever brighter till the full light of day. But the way of the wicked is like deep darkness.

—Proverbs 4:18–19

AVOID

KEEPING THE SECRETS

Bring Your Family into Light

Stanley stood up as the group emerged from the room down the hall. Surrounding his wife and daughters, a phalanx of lawyers and state workers parted bystanders to the right and left. Betty wouldn't even look at him. Neither would Sarah, his youngest. Lizzie, however, kept her eyes on him the entire walk down the hall. Her face was a blank mask, but her eyes burned right through him.

Yep, she was going to be trouble, that one. Always had been. As soon as she'd figured out that he was doing with Sarah what he'd been doing with her, she actually threatened him. Told him she'd tell if he kept it up. Her face had looked the same way back then.

She'd become too much like him, he guessed. Stubborn. There'd been no telling what she'd say, so he hadn't wanted to risk it. Never thought it'd end up like this. Hanging the family laundry out for everyone to see, to judge. It wasn't like he'd hurt them or anything. Why, look at them; they were just fine. Fine enough to walk right past him, ready to call him names in front of strangers.

Finally, his lawyer finished his phone calls and approached him, walking quickly. Taking him by the arm, the kid began to hustle him into the courtroom. As hard and cold as that bench had been, Stanley suddenly realized he'd rather sit there all day than have to go through the next few hours. No one was going to listen to him, or believe him, or try to understand his side of the story. He was going to get lynched, plain and simple. And his family was supplying the rope.

Stories like this one should never happen. No child should have to go through the emotional devastation of having to accuse a loved one of terrible acts against them. Trust should never be ravaged, especially not within families. Children should never have to live in fear of the very people who are supposed to love and protect them. A kiss at bedtime from a parent should be given out of love, not perversion. A gathering of aunts and uncles, cousins and far-flung family should bring thoughts of joy, not of dread.

No, it was never supposed to be like that. Then sin entered the world and darkness followed.

"Everyone who does evil hates the light, and will not come into the light for fear that his deeds will be exposed," Jesus said. Was he talking about Stanley? The coin does have another side. "Whoever lives by the truth comes into the light, so that it may be seen plainly that what he has done has been done through God" (John 3:20–21).

How an Abuser Turns Up the Heat

People who sexually victimize children have a definite pattern to their behavior—a pattern often observed by therapists and law-enforcement officials. It is not unlike the pattern of the sexual manipulator. In both instances, the desired result is their own sexual gratification, either through inappropriate conversation, physical touching, or sexual activity. This pattern is distinctive. If you were abused as a child, as you read over this pattern, analyze it in light of your own past. It is important for you to know that what happened to you was deliberate, calculated, and planned. Your actions did not cause it, did not hasten it, did not provoke it. No matter how you actually felt during the abuse, you were a victim of sexual abuse, not a participant in sexual activity.

God's word clearly calls this kind of sexual activity sin. The bodies of our children were not given to us as objects to appease our lust. Even the non-Christians in our culture tend to agree with the Bible's prohibition on sex between blood kin. God says, "No one is to approach any close relative to have sexual relations. I am the LORD" (Leviticus 18:6). Thus to be sure we understand, the prohibited sexual relationships are listed. According to this passage, a man should never have sex with:

1. His mother
2. His father's wife
3. His sister
4. His niece
5. His half sister
6. His aunt
7. His aunt by marriage
8. His daughter-in-law
9. His brother's wife
10. A woman and her daughter
11. His wife's nieces
12. The sister of a living wife
13. A menstruating woman
14. His neighbor's wife
15. Any other male
16. Any animal

Notice that right along with bestiality, adultery, and homosexual sex, God lists sex between family members, and he calls such behavior "detestable" (Leviticus 18:26). If someone in your family has forced sex on you, that person has done a detestable thing. He has sinned against you. You are not the sinner. The offender is.

Thankfully, not everyone who reads this book will have a history of incestuous abuse. Still it is important for you to be aware of the usual stages of sexual aggression. You need to be informed if you suspect someone within your family of acting in an inappropriately sexual way toward someone else in the family. Understanding the pattern can provide you with a foundation to assess suspicious behavior.

Choosing a Victim

The first step for the sexual predator within the family is generally to evaluate potential victims just as Amnon targeted Tamar his sister. The predator may be looking for a specific gender, age, disposition, or simply, availability. If no victim is found within the immediate family, the sexual predator may look to the extended family, whether blood related or blended.

When the potential victim has been identified, the sexual predator will begin to whittle down the natural barriers children have against sexual and sexually violent behavior. The younger the child, the fewer the barriers. The younger the child, the more inherent their trust of the adult. Younger children may be won over to the predator's side by tangible gifts and/or expressions of love and acceptance. Just by showing the child attention an adult can offer tremendous incentive for the child to do whatever is necessary to continue such a relationship with the adult. At first, the predator is attentive and giving, making the child feel special. And they are. The predator has chosen this child especially for acts of violation and abuse.

After the child has been softened up to be kindly disposed toward the adult, the predator will often begin exploration of what the child will tolerate sexually. The predator may begin interjecting sexual phrases or words into private conversation with the child. Usually at this stage the predator begins to take advantage of opportunities to abuse times of normal family physical contact such as kissing, hugging, patting on the back, holding hands, or sitting on a lap. During these physical displays, the predator will extend the contact. Gestures that communicate love in healthy family relationships become expressions of lust when offered by a predator, but a naive, young victim may not yet discern the crucial difference.

Initially, the predator stays in the protection mode, even while stalking the younger prey. If the child objects to the contact and tells another adult or family member, the predator has a built-in excuse for what happened. The inappropriate extension remains camouflaged by the appropriate activity.

Often this interjection of doubt is just what the family is hoping for. Nobody wants the abuse to be true and if another, more reasonable, less disturbing explanation can be given, many people will choose to assume the child misunderstood or misread the intentions of the adult. And the child can often be talked into this benign assessment of the behavior to which they objected.

If the charade works, the predator then has a decision to make. Should they continue to pursue this victim or should they look elsewhere for their perverted sexual gratification? Usually this depends upon the demeanor of the child. If the child continues to insist that the behavior is wrong, the predator will usually go elsewhere. In some cases, the child may refuse to have anything more to do with the predator. The possibility of discovery is then far greater than if the child continues to be confused.

If the child has either been convinced of the harmlessness of the act or is confused about what really happened, the predator will often strike again during this vulnerable time. The child, even while protesting, may not risk the same reaction again from the other family members. In essence, the denial of the family the first time around protects not the child but the predator, preserving the aura of secrecy the predator wants to achieve to hide the abuse of the child. Silence and denial by the family leave the child more vulnerable to the predator's subsequent advances.

Culminating the Abuse

When the predator has the victim firmly in the control, the illicit activity the predator has been working toward will take place. In some instances, the predator is grooming the child for acts of sexual intercourse. But this is not always the case. Sexual abuse can take place even if the child does not suffer penetration, either vaginally or anally. The predator may be grooming the child to perform oral sex. In these cases the predator's goal is to use the child as a provider for their own sexual stimulation and physical culmination.

Sometimes the predator's main interest is inappropriate conversations or physical touching. Because of the circumstances of the contact between predator and victim, or because of the constraints of the predator, the inappropriate behavior may be highly opportunistic and situational. In any event, the predator's behavior is perverted. To engage a child or adolescent in sexualized behavior, especially taking advantage of a familial relationship, is wrong. Whether the predator uses the child to verbalize sexualized thoughts and fantasies, to engage in inappropriate sexual touching, or to participate in overt sexual activity, we are talking about sinful behavior God detests.

Predators are meeting their own perverted needs when they choose to victimize a child. In some cases the sexual gratification of the predator comes from their ability to sexually arouse the child. Their ability to control the physical, sexual response of the child is the sexual trigger they use to bring about their own physical gratification. This kind of abuse can be especially devastating to the child. Predators use their victims' own bodies against them. If

Tamar actually enjoyed her time in Amnon's bed, his sin against her was double, for this would make her blame herself for his sin. Mentally and emotionally the child may dread the sexual interaction with a predator, but physically the victim's body is being manipulated to respond. This response fortifies the argument of the adult about the harmless nature of the activity. "How did I hurt her?" the predator may ask. "She enjoyed it." The "enjoyment" produces overwhelming guilt in the child and increases the child's motivation to keep the behavior secret.

Showing True Colors

After the predator has captured the child sexually, the facade of relationship is no longer necessary. The predator's main goal now is to keep the child under control in order to facilitate future abuse and to hide past abuse. Threats, both physical and psychological, will often be employed by the predator to ensure compliance, concealment, and complicity.

The overriding feature of each step of the victimization of the child is secrecy. Only in secret can most of this abuse take place. It must be kept secret from family, associates, and society at large. Predators hate the light of exposure, for it reveals the true nature of their actions and the depravity of their souls.

Come into the Light

Because of the trust inherent in the family relationship, most people recoil at the very notion that a father could be abusing his daughter, or an aunt could be abusing her nephew, or a grandfather could be abusing his grandson. If we are sexually sane, it makes our stomachs turn and our minds retreat. We don't want it to be true. A part of us wants to be kept in the dark about such things. We want to close our eyes and think, *If I can't see it, it doesn't exist.* King David chose to act like the prince's abuse of the princess never happened. He was like many parents today. The only problem with this approach is that when we open our eyes, the horrid mess is still there.

When you open your eyes, is it still there for you?

DEALING WITH PAST ABUSE

The loving relationship expected within a family is perverted by the sexual aggressor to include attitudes and actions God never intended. Children are to be nurtured and loved in the family, not exploited and abused.

Children grow up, of course. Even abused children. As adults, the victims need to come to grips with both the sexual abuse they suffered as well as their feelings regarding that abuse. Past abuse needs to be dealt with in the present so that it does not devastate the future.

Denying the Past Won't Make It Go Away

Many people who have been exposed to an inappropriately sexualized family relationship as a child feel they just need to get on with their lives as an adult. A part of them recognizes what happened to them as a child, but they may choose not to consciously deal with it. They see the abuse as a fact of the past with little or no effect in the present. As a child, they compartmentalized their feelings during the abuse in order to cope. As an adult, the compartmentalization may continue as they wall off the experiences within their mind. Again, if they don't acknowledge it to themselves, they can operate as if it really didn't happen or was not as damaging as it seemed at the time.

Often the abuse tapers off or ends as the child grows older. The sexual aggressor may find another, younger family member to exploit. The child may establish a greater sense of will and understanding, making them more resistant to the manipulations of the sexual aggressor. The exploitation becomes less frequent although the relationship with the sexual aggressor continues within the family. An older brother who abuses a younger sister when she is six or seven may move away from the family, thus ending the intimate opportunity for abuse. The brother and sister remain in relationship because of their family connection, but the abusive pattern has been altered. Over time, the temptation on the part of both the older brother and the younger sister may be to pretend the whole thing didn't happen or was just childish exploration. After all, who wants to admit that things like this take place in their family?

Denial does not equate to removal. Denied feelings still must be experienced to be denied. You cannot deny something that does not exist. Denying the truth of a situation, even an inappropriately sexualized family relationship, does not stop the emotional damage as a victim grows up. Only acceptance of the truth allows all the pieces to be put into place. As Jesus promised, the truth sets us free from slavery to sin (John 8:31–32). Facing the truth about our past can set us free from the enslavement of family secrets.

Each of us is a compilation of our experiences. Nobody's past is compiled of strictly pleasant, beneficial experiences. Each of us must deal with the tragic, the devastating, the disappointing in our lives. Dealing with these negative experiences and integrating them into who we are as adults crafts our character. If we avoid dealing with these emotions, we stunt our ability to mature into well-rounded people.

Assessing Proper Blame Instead of Accepting Guilt

Children live in a world confused by the actions and explanations of the adults they depend on. One way kids control this confusion is to make themselves responsible for adult actions. In cases of divorce, children will often assume they are to blame for their parents' breakup. Somehow the situation seems more in control if it happens because of something they have done. If their actions caused the divorce, they reason, their actions should be able to bring their parents back together. Accepting guilt is one way we try to gain control over a chaotic, incomprehensible series of events.

This may explain in part why children who have been victimized by an inappropriately sexualized family relationship feel so guilty about that abuse. Subconsciously they may assume that if the abuse was caused by their actions, then they should be able to do something to stop it. This gives them a sense of control over the problem.

From an objective distance, you and I can see, of course, that this is a false sense of control. When they are unable to stop the abuse, this false control leads to even more false guilt. The sense of control that shielded them from chaos as a child can burden them with crippling guilt as adults. As a child, they tell themselves, they should have done more to stop it. They should have told someone about it. They should have told someone else about it. They should have taken matters into their own hands, somehow, and defended themselves more vigorously. As a child, they should have but didn't. The "didn't" causes guilt and shame that can be overwhelming.

If the improper sexual interaction produced a physical reaction from the child, the later guilt is even greater. They assume they must participate in the blame because they participated in the physical pleasure of the sexual behavior. Indictment comes through their own sexual response to the abuse.

In cases where children are sexually abused by older family members, however, the real guilt and shame belong to the sexual aggressor. This person alone is to blame for the abuse. The victim deserves no part in the guilt or the blame.

Taking Back Control

As terrible as it is, some who read this book are living the nightmare of familial sexual abuse. This book is not addressed to young people, but we include the next few lines just in case a youthful victim has read this far. Please seek help. Do not allow the abuse to continue in silence.

First, speak to a trusted adult, such as a parent, about the abuse.

If your abuser is a parent, speak to another trusted adult, such as another family member, a school counselor, a religious advisor, or a law-enforcement officer.

If the adult you've chosen to speak to does not believe you, do not stop. Seek out another trusted adult until you find someone who *will* believe you.

Be prepared to explain, in detail, the nature of the abuse you have suffered. It is rarely enough just to say you have been abused. While reciting the facts will undoubtedly be difficult, it is important for you to be able to articulate what has happened. The person you go to for help will need to understand the nature and depth of the abuse so they can better counsel you and take appropriate action.

Remember, as you explain what has happened to you, you are not to blame.

The Light Shining, Not Blinding

If the sexual offenses within a family lie in the past, the most powerful weapon the abuser has is the secrecy that covers the truth of their actions. Keeping the secrets of the family by pretending it never happened or never talking about it empowers the abuser and weakens the abused. The most effective way to regain control over the abuse is to expose it to the light.

But whom do you tell? Who is it that needs to know about the abuse and the identity of the family member who abused you?

1. The abused needs to know. They need to understand that what happened to them was wrong. They need to understand that they are not to blame for what happened.

2. The abuser needs to know. They need to understand what their actions have meant. They need to be held accountable for the consequences of those actions. They need to be confronted with the wrong they have done.

3. Those who are vulnerable need to know. If the abuser has a pattern of predatory action against certain family members, those family members need to know. They need to know so they or the adults responsible for them can determine if contact with the abuser will even be permitted. Depending on the type and severity of action, merely avoiding being alone with the abuser may be enough to forestall any abuse. However, the degree of contact allowed is completely up to the other family members. The abuser, family member or not, has broken the trust of the family and has no right to demand any in the future. Blood may be thicker than water, but no blood is thick enough to cover the consequences of familial abuse.

If no family members are currently in danger from the abuser, the question of who should know comes down to why they should know. For example, what if the abuser was an uncle, now dead, who made it a habit to trap his nieces in inappropriate hugs accompanied by coarse jokes or suggestions? Why should his widow be told of his abusive pattern now? His death precludes any reoccurrence. No one else needs protection from his actions. While the nieces can certainly gain strength by talking to each other about their shared experiences, of what value is it to tell his widow? The Bible does teach us to speak "the truth in love" (Ephesians 4:15).

The light of truth should be used to illuminate the dark places. It is not meant as a weapon to blind others. Shining the light of truth should facilitate healing in the family, not bring about further wounds. "Let your light shine before men, that they may see your good deeds and praise your Father in heaven," Jesus bid us (Matthew 5:16). When shining the light of truth before men, remember the desired outcome: that they will see what you do and praise God because of it.

When You Decide to Confront

If you have been abused by someone in your family, the time may come when you feel compelled to stop keeping the secret and to confront your abuser. This is not a decision someone else can make for you. Only you can determine when and if that time has come.

You can go about confronting that person several ways, depending on your comfort level.

1. Alone. You can decide to confront in person, alone. It may be important for you to look your abuser straight in the face as you explain what their actions have meant to you. Most of those who have been abused, however, will not choose this option. Even being within the same vicinity as their abuser brings up past feelings of helplessness and rage. Most will choose to confront another way.

Going to the abuser alone could prove physically dangerous. Depending on the strength of the abuser and of their denial, their desperation to keep their dark secrets hidden could motivate them to physical violence or verbal abuse. The benefits of confronting your abuser may not outweigh the dangers of confronting them alone.

2. With friends. The Scriptures offer us wise counsel on this. "Though one may be overpowered, two can defend themselves. A cord of three strands is not quickly broken" (Ecclesiastes 4:12). If you decide to confront an abuser in person, take along family or friends. If your abuse included acts of violence, it may be unwise to ever be alone again with the aggressor.

Take people with you who will allow you to do the confronting and who won't try to do your job for you. The purpose of their presence at the confrontation is to protect you while you speak, to ensure your thoughts are expressed, and to provide you with their strength.

Clearly this is not a job for a casual friend. Choose someone you know to be reliable, discreet, and steadfast. Confrontation is rarely pleasant, and almost never in circumstances such as this. Do not choose individuals who will need your support during the intensity of the confrontation.

3. Over the telephone. If you are not comfortable with confronting in person, you might try talking to your abuser over the telephone. You have no guarantee, however, that the abuser will continue to listen to you on the other end. They may decide to hang up.

4. In writing. Some victims decide to confront their abusers through the written word. Sitting down and composing a letter to your abuser may give you sufficient time and presence of mind to frame your thoughts to maximum effect. In a letter, it is you putting forth your thoughts. You are not required to respond to the thoughts of the other person. It is not necessary for you to defend, to argue, to convince. In a letter, you are laying out your feelings. It is the abuser's responsibility alone to decide how to respond.

Putting Out the Fire by Forgiving

Anger, resentment, and shame are powerful emotions. Left unchecked, they can become a fire that can consume a person. Whether an abuser ever acknowledges wrong actions or asks for forgiveness, often the only way for the abused to go on is to bestow forgiveness. By choosing to forgive you take back control over your life.

The terrible things that happen to us should not constitute the sole content of our character.

We are more than that.

Our lives should be defined as more than the worst things we've ever had to endure.

Life is greater than that.

Our view should be broader than the negative aspects of our experiences.

Our horizons are wider than that.

Our identities as people should include more than how other people choose to see us.

Our God is bigger than that.

Instead of bottling up the secrets of the past, perhaps it is time to allow the light of truth to shine into your life. Instead of harboring rage and resentment, perhaps it is time to allow for healing in your life. Instead of concentrating solely on the abuse of your past, perhaps it is time to refocus on the salvation of your present and future.

——— Fuel for Thought ———

This chapter has undoubtedly been difficult to read. It was not easy to write. The concept of a loving family should be a reality for every person. Because of sin, it is not. This truth grieves God more than anyone. He sees and knows the consequences of sin within families. In his love for us, he has provided us with another family to furnish what our earthly families so often cannot. Within God's family, with him as our Father and Christ as our Brother, we can join together in their perfect love. Surrounded by the love of God's family, may you find strength to come to terms with the hurts of your family on earth.

1. If you were abused by a family member in the past, have you ever told anyone? If so, whom? If not, why?

2. If there were one thing you could say to a family member who abused you, what would it be?

3. What are your greatest fears about having the truth about the past come to light?

4. Do you feel somehow responsible for bad things that happened to you?

5. If you were abused as a child, have you confronted your abuser? If so, what happened when you did?

6. If you have not confronted your abuser, do you think a time will come when you will be able to? What are you waiting for?

7. Given the type of abuse, which other family members do you feel need to know?

8. Have you forgiven your abuser? If so, how does this make you feel? If not, what would need to happen for you to be able to?

9. Go over the account of the rape of Tamar. List the names of the family members who were aware of her abuse. How were family relationships damaged because of Amnon's sin?

Helpful Resource: The damage done by inappropriately sexualized family relationships is significant. While reading this chapter, you may have realized that behavior you have been either denying or minimizing shows the pattern of a sexual predator. For more information on this sensitive subject, consider reading the book *The Wounded Heart: Hope for Adult Victims of Childhood Sexual Abuse* by Dr. Dan B. Allender. Whatever you do, please keep letting in the light as you feel able. Even if it is only one ray at a time.

MAY GOD BIND UP YOUR WOUNDS *and give your soul peace. May he empower you through his Spirit to find the ability to forgive and move forward with your life.*

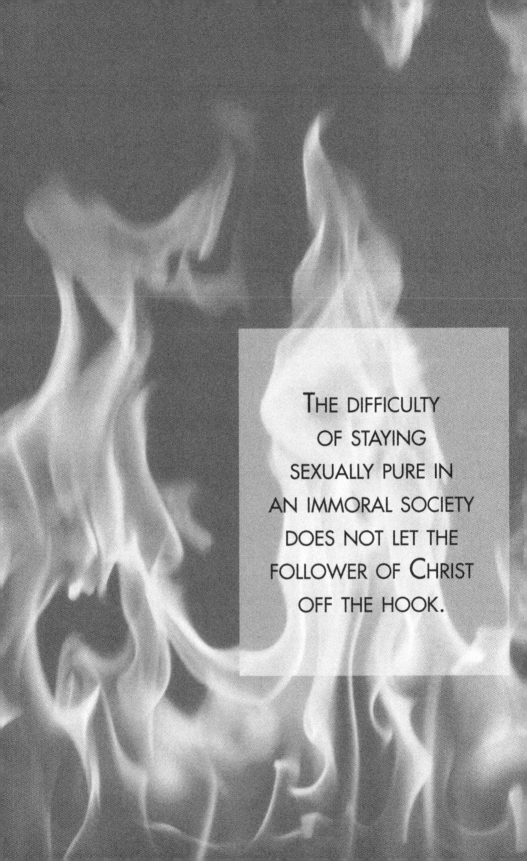

THE DIFFICULTY
OF STAYING
SEXUALLY PURE IN
AN IMMORAL SOCIETY
DOES NOT LET THE
FOLLOWER OF CHRIST
OFF THE HOOK.

9

RECOGNIZE

THE POWER OF COMPANIONSHIP

Friendships Can Lead to Inappropriate Intimacy

Jeff jumped into his Celica and punched it down the freeway. He wanted to make sure he got to the game in time to take in some batting practice. It had been awhile since he played, more than a few years, and Jeff didn't want to be fanning air when he got up to bat the first time.

After his divorce Jeff had kind of gone overboard working all the time. One of the guys at work, Dave, asked him if he'd like to play on his team. One of their players got transferred right at the start of the season, and Dave remembered Jeff saying he'd played in high school. Why not, Jeff thought. It wasn't like he had anything but an empty apartment to go home to after work.

The first game was great. Jeff plastered a double in the third and a two-run triple in the seventh to give his team a lead. Everyone had cheered, slapping him on the back and talking about "the ringer" Dave had brought. It felt great, being part of a team and being appreciated. Jeff hated to admit it, but feeling appreciated was one of the things he missed most from his failed marriage. Not that Shelley had appreciated him much toward the end, but she had during those first years. It had been nice.

Meeting Beth was pretty nice too. She played third base on the team. Attractive and funny, she was always encouraging other team members. Jeff asked Dave about her at work the next day. Dave said Beth had been playing on the team for three years, the first two with her husband, Rob. Beth and Rob were going through a tough time right now, Dave confided. Rob was going back to school and had classes on most of the nights they had games. The two of them weren't really getting along. Dave admitted he'd been relieved when Rob decided not to play for the season.

Having just gone through a divorce, Jeff certainly could relate to Beth's marital struggles. The last six months with Shelley had been tough. Maybe underneath that bubbly personality Beth was hurting as much as he was. Maybe she needed someone to talk to. Maybe all she needed was a friend.

No doubt you have heard the phrase "The road to hell is paved with good intentions." Most of us start out our friendships with the best of intentions. We desire connection with someone else. We look for someone who will understand and accept us just the way we are. We look for someone we can share with and care about. We intend for our friendships to be holy, healthy, aboveboard relationships.

The exception to this, of course, is the sexual predator, manipulator, or climber. For them, connection is important only for what they can get out of the relationship. In fact, the relationships they form cannot really be called friendships. Friendships are based on the mutual affection and respect of those involved. The intimacy and sexual rewards sought by these individuals are false and misleading. Presenting the illusion of friendship, they actually seek only their own selfish gain. They offer what most other people desire for the express purpose of attaining only what they desire.

The allure of compassion and companionship is powerful. Friendships based on sharing and caring can be some of the most satisfying. What could be wrong with wanting that? Nothing. But satisfaction gained in an emotional sense can sometimes lead to a desire to gain satisfaction in a sexual sense. If the friendship already is providing a variety of basic emotional needs, the temptation to expand the friendship into a sexual realm can be powerful. Flirtation and sexual tension are intoxicating stimulants. Carried too far, what starts out with the best of intentions can result in the worst of ramifications.

DATING AND COURTSHIP

Within the courtship process two people spend a great deal of time simply getting to know one another, each person exploring the character, personality, and emotional makeup of the other. When dating, each person begins to connect with the other. Trying each other on for size, they determine just how well they fit as a couple.

During this time, when information and thoughts are shared, the daters become more and more comfortable with each other. The stilted formality of the first few dates is substituted by a growing familiarity and ease around each other. Emotional bonding takes place. They become friends. If you've been there, you know the process.

Up to this point nothing is wrong. This is what dating and courtship is for. We no longer live in a time or a culture of arranged marriages. Each person determines who their friends will be. Each person determines who they will date, court, and eventually, marry. Some people date a lot of friends over an extended period. Some of us are quickly smitten by Cupid, and our dating days soon end at the marriage altar. But most of us have some experience in the game we call dating.

Through this dating process, men and women are coming together, bonding together. Falling in and out of friendship. Falling in and out of love. They are taking the steps necessary to determine the strength of their bonds and the depth of their commitment to each other.

By definition dating involves romance. It implies some level of sexual attraction. But it also implies clear sexual boundaries. Dating is not marriage. It is a possible prelude to marriage, but the sexual intimacies of marriage are out of place in dating relationships. If the emotional intimacy between two daters leads to physical intimacy, the relationship has become inappropriately sexualized.

Not everyone agrees with this assessment, not that their argument matters. Only one assessment has any validity. Since God created male and female and sexuality, it is his call which relationships may be sexualized. A male-female relationship outside of marriage isn't one. On this Scriptures are plain.

If it were left to us, all of us would rationalize our own aberrant behavior. Sexuality is a powerful phenomenon. God specifically designed it that way. Exercised in righteousness, it provides the linchpin for many happy marriages. Debased in sin, it leads to lust and perversion. The power is the same, whether used for righteousness or sin. Our human capacity for denial and rationalization makes the judgment between which is righteousness and which is sin often impossible to decide. Thanks be to God that he keeps that judgment unto himself! Thanks be to God that he reveals to us in his word what his decision is!

You might be tempted at this point to object. You might be tempted to ask something like the following: Doesn't God understand how difficult sexual purity is? Doesn't he know about the pressure to have sex in this culture today? Doesn't he realize staying pure goes against what everybody else says to do?

The answer is yes, of course God knows. Of course he is aware of the type of world we live in today. His answer is found in 1 Corinthians 7:2: "Since there is so much immorality, each man should have his own wife, and each woman her own husband." The secret to staying sexually pure is to make a decision to abstain from a sexualized relationship until you get married. Resolve to save sex for that relationship.

The difficulty of staying sexually pure in an immoral society does not let the follower of Christ off the hook. During the course of human history, other societies have degraded themselves through sexual depravity. They were not let off the hook by God. On the contrary, two of them, Sodom and Gomorrah, were utterly destroyed by God because of their evil.

FRIENDS ONLY

Have you ever known two people—a man and a woman—who became extraordinarily close friends? Nobody who knew them attributed even a hint of sexuality to their relationship. On the highest, holiest level they were friends. Platonic friends. Because of their shared interest and complementary personalities, they found a special delight in each other's company.

A friendship like this is rare enough to be remarkable, even if it exists between two same-sex friends. But this sort of nonsexualized bond between a woman and a man is truly unique—partly because our society offers few acceptable venues for such a relationship to flower, and partly because so few human beings could keep such an emotionally intimate relationship from mutating eventually into something romantic and sexual at the core.

Some respectable therapists postulate that the likelihood of a relationship turning sexual rises alarmingly in proportion to the hours a man and a woman spend in close proximity. The more cynical experts insist that sexual feelings will be stirred and sexual union likely will occur if the man and woman work together alone more than a certain number of hours. They don't even have to be friends. They don't have to like each other. The basic male/female attraction wired into our biology makes the result predictable.

What if you do like each other? What does the emotional bonding of "friends only" contribute to the likelihood that one day, despite best intentions, sexual boundaries will crumble and treasured commitments to other relationships will be lost. The risk escalates if either of the two friends hits a rocky time in their marriage or gets knocked off balance by an emotional trauma.

Wise people who honor God's sex-in-marriage-only rule will be careful to limit opposite-sex friendships to settings that involve spouses and other friends. Even then high-octane emotional intimacy is best saved for one's mate.

WHAT GOD HAS JOINED TOGETHER

As people in today's culture wait longer to marry and as men and women interact more and more apart from a family context, male and female friendships can occur even when one or both are married to someone else. Again, nothing is inherently wrong with men and women having friends of the opposite sex while married. But the situation is filled with risk.

The danger is for the friendship to be viewed as a place to augment needs either neglected or ignored by the marriage of one or both of the friends. The danger is for the friendship to become the primary relationship, superseding the marriage relationship.

Friendships, by nature, are a comfortable place to be. They offer warmth, acceptance, relaxation, and fun. All of these are present without the component of sexual relations adding tension and uncertainty. In a male-female friendship all of these are present, along with the acknowledgment of gender. This acknowledgment of gender contributes to a sense of sexual awareness, even if the friendship is not sexual. Someone may say, "Oh, Lisa is just like one of the guys," but she's not and they know it. Someone may say, "Why, talking to Bill is like talking with one of my girlfriends," but it isn't and they know it. Within this comfortable platform of openness and acceptance, the temptation to shift a personal boundary can easily surface. The very openness and acceptance that make the friendship valuable also make it dangerous. One slip can invite disaster.

Not all husbands and wives enjoy a relationship where they adequately respond to the needs or wants of each other. They may be joined together by God, but as a couple they are lagging behind. Because of patterns they have seen in their own families, they may neglect or ignore certain needs of their spouse. Out of ignorance of how men and women relate differently to each other, they may seek to satisfy only those needs they have in common, ignoring an entire range of gender-based thoughts and emotions.

Friendships fill this void. When the friendship is a male-female one, the friends may either look to each other to fill those gaps or to explain why those gaps exist. How many inappropriate relationships have started out with the words, "Maybe you can help me understand my husband/wife?"

When the male-female friendship becomes more comfortable and more responsive than the marriage relationship, the former can quickly take precedence over the latter. If a choice is to be made between spending time with the friend or the spouse, the friendship wins. If a choice is to be made about where to go to get a need met, the friendship wins. Under these circumstances, if the friendship wins, the marriage loses.

Too often, friends within a friendship can begin to look at the absent spouse in an "us versus them" mode. This is especially true if one of the activities of the friendship is to talk about, complain about, commiserate about one or both of the spouses. Since the friends consider themselves as a unit, as an "us," spouses get bumped into the "them" category. And the spouse generally isn't around to present his or her point of view or to reinforce spousal identity. Just as an "us versus them" mind-set makes workplace partners more vulnerable to sexual attraction, so it can put friends at risk.

Friends stick up for each other. Like the three musketeers, their attitude is "All for one and one for all." So if one of the friends is perceived as being injured by the absent spouse, the present friend rushes to the defense, declaring, in essence, "I'd never do anything like that to you!" or, "I don't understand how they could act that way!" At least for that moment the commiserating friend assumes the place of a substitute spouse. What happens momentarily can become permanent when friends replace spouses.

EMOTIONAL ADULTERY

Male and female friends, where one or both of the friends is married, need to be exceedingly careful how much they bond emotionally. This bonding, if carried too deep, could become emotional adultery. In this case no physical adultery occurs, but the friendship displaces the marriage as the primary source for emotional contact and expression. And it doesn't take a genius to know then that physical adultery is not far behind. The potential for boundaries to shift and fall in this situation demands that men and women enter into relationships in general, and friendships in particular, with wisdom and truth.

Because emotional adultery stops short of physical intimacy, it is often easier for a person to rationalize and allow. We are wrong, however, if we think that filling an emotional need is not as powerful a motivation as filling a physical one. We are physical beings, yes, but we are also highly emotional ones. For some men and most women, the fulfillment of emotional needs is paramount to the filling of physical ones. When our intimate emotional needs are being satisfied by someone other than our spouse, our marriage bonds may be stretched beyond their limit.

When marriages are shattered by an affair, the primary reason for the spouse to stray is companionship and affection. Sexual activity is certainly part of the infidelity, but the affair often begins because somebody has an ear willing to listen and a broad shoulder to lean on.

THE DANGER OF FALSE INTIMACY

We've observed that male-female friendships can lead to inappropriate intimacy between the two friends, and we've noted that the inappropriate intimacy can be emotional intimacy or it can be actual, physical intimacy. But another type of intimacy is also inappropriate. It is false intimacy. False intimacy exists within a relationship when the care and concern expressed by one or both of the people involved is an illusion.

This illusion can be created in two ways. The first is through a deliberate attempt to create a facade of concern for the express purpose of taking advantage of the other person. We have seen that sexual aggressors, manipulators, and climbers use false intimacy to create a camouflage of care behind which they can hide their true intentions.

Intimacy can be false if it is established without a solid basis of shared experiences and mutual trust. This can happen if casual relationships get fast-forwarded into personal or intimate realms. The rate or level of sharing may outpace the normal flow of relationships, which must grow and deepen over time. These intense, "hot" relationships have a tendency to flame brightly and burn out quickly, like tumbleweeds on a campfire. Eventually the two people realize the relationship has no solid foundation, just momentary intensity.

THE DANGER OF ONLINE RELATIONSHIPS

While false intimacy has always been a danger in male-female relationships, the recent emergence of cyberspace friendships has allowed this condition to proliferate. We discussed some Internet dangers earlier, particularly the obvious risks in online pornography and temptations of online anonymity. Consider for a moment how easily this medium confuses relationships by introducing the element of false intimacy.

Chapter 9

Rita couldn't wait to get home. At work she kept checking her watch, counting down the hours. Part of her giggled at her foolishness, but she didn't care. She had a date. And the best part was she didn't have to worry about what she was going to wear or how her hair looked or whether she could get into her "skinny" jeans. Her date, Jeff, would never know the difference. Jeff was an online date.

Hopping onto her favorite chat room one night, she'd gotten into an in-depth discussion with someone named "Carl" about the differences between men and women. Carl had been complaining about the last few women he'd dated and was, basically, blasting anyone female. Naturally, Rita had risen to the challenge and vigorously defended her gender. Carl, no rocket scientist, hadn't been able to keep up with her rapid-fire repartee, but their give-and-take attracted a crowd. Before long, several others had joined in, on one side or the other. The discussion got quite heated and sarcastic.

After several hours, participants began to drop off, citing other obligations, disgust with the content in general, or understandably, fatigue. It had been a Thursday night, and Rita had every other Friday off, so she stayed on late. She had nothing better to do, and she really loved the freedom of spilling her guts online. Flaming Carl the Cretin was so much fun. He came across as some sort of Neanderthal. Served him right.

One by one, the other participants faded out, even Carl. Finally, it was just her and a guy named Jeff. He hadn't said a lot when the fur was flying, preferring to interject comments only occasionally. She remembered being impressed by his short, pithy responses. Somehow he seemed to really understand women without losing his masculinity. Rita was drawn to him like a magnet.

The connection made that night had continued between them now for more than three months. Thursdays seemed to be a good night for Jeff to go online, though he never told her why. Going into work on the Fridays she worked was hard after spending hours online, but Rita didn't care. Sharing with Jeff was really incredible.

He was so interested in her. What did she think? What would she do? What was happening in her life? He didn't seem to mind if she rattled on and on.

About himself, though, Jeff wasn't quite so forthcoming. His silence gave him an aura of mystery. Rita could imagine him any way she chose. After all, what did it really matter what color his hair was, how old he was, or what his collar size was? By not knowing these specifics, Rita had the freedom to think of him as a thin intellectual one day, or a burly athlete the next, or a tousled-haired artist after that.

It was really up to her, because Jeff rarely wanted to talk about himself. He seemed to prefer letting her be the focus of their conversations. After some of the guys Rita had gone out with, this was a breath of fresh air. Rita couldn't think of anything about herself she hadn't shared in the past three months.

In a way, it was like talking to one of her girlfriends: no holds barred, only better.

Welcome to the future of dating. Only it's here now, and some people are finding it's not all it's cracked up to be. The Internet used to be the primary domain of computer geeks and techno-nerds. Not anymore. Millions of people now have access to the Internet, with hundreds more going online literally every day.

Some of the most popular mediums on the information superhighway are chat rooms, bulletin boards, and e-mail servers. These forums are highly interactive. Participants can communicate easily and anonymously.

It is the anonymity of Internet communications that can lead to false intimacy. After reading the scenario above, it might seem to you that Rita's feelings for Jeff are genuine, based on their time together online. All they're doing is getting to know each other, you might say. Why, it's no different than sitting in a restaurant and sharing who you are and what you hope for your life.

But instead of talking back and forth, they're typing back and forth. Instead of actually sitting side by side, they're sitting individually at their own computers. They're connected in cyberspace, but is that enough?

With anonymity comes a loosening of the bonds of accountability. If someone doesn't know who you are, you can't be held accountable for what you say. Why not go ahead and talk about a subject you'd normally avoid? If someone doesn't know who you are, why not create a new, different identity? Who's to know?

What if Jeff isn't who Rita thinks he is? What if *Jeff* isn't his real name? What if he is a fifty-eight-year-old married father of three, grandfather of four? What if he has no intention of ever telling Rita anything about himself? What if his whole purpose for corresponding with Rita is her willingness to share personal information about her life? What if his whole purpose is to draw Rita into an escalating dialogue of intimate details? What if Rita is eagerly awaiting conversing with someone who actually cares nothing about her personally but has only voyeuristic interest in the personal, even sexual, aspects of her life? He could be a cyber equivalent of a Peeping Tom, watching Rita "undress" from a distance to satisfy his own prurient needs.

What if Jeff isn't who Rita thinks he is? What if he is a thirty-six year old convicted con man? What if his whole purpose for drawing Rita out in intimate, personal communication is to gain her trust so he can rip her off financially?

What if Jeff is exactly who he says, which isn't much? How is Rita to know?

That's the problem with Internet communications: You have no way to know. You really don't know the person you are corresponding with on e-mail or conversing with in a chat room or on a bulletin board. They might be who they say they are; then again, they might not. And the intimacy gained from a lengthy online relationship could be a prelude to taking advantage of the online partner.

The intimacy gained from an online relationship could also be a result of diving headfirst into heady, personal waters without checking the depth of the bottom first. Internet communications, concealed by the separation inherent in cyberspace, often take on highly personal, sexual content. Questions and responses people would never consider exchanging offline even with good friends hit the Internet with a few impersonal, detached strokes of the keyboard. Words that would never be uttered aloud flow off of fingertips with only the slightest hesitation. The more the words and thoughts are typed, the easier they become to share. The Internet, then, becomes a fast track to false intimacy.

—— Fuel for Thought ——

We humans are social creatures. We need and enjoy the companionship of others. A life of solitude disconnected from others is not one most of us would willingly choose. Instead, we venture out into the world and form friendships with those around us.

God knows we need compassion and human companionship. He designed friendships between people to provide for our needs. God knows we need emotional and physical connection. He designed the marriage relationship to fill those needs. The challenge for male-female friendships is to avoid confusing the two.

God knows we need compassion and divine companionship. He designed a garden where we could walk and talk with him. God knows we are unable to maintain our connection with him because of the sin in our lives. He designed a cross to bridge the gap between us and him, to bring us to him in love and forgiveness.

God himself desires connection and companionship with us. This is, perhaps, one of the greatest mysteries in Scripture. From the very foundation of the world it has always been God's plan to provide for fellowship with him and companionship with those around us. His plan makes it possible. His word makes it clear. Our obedience makes it holy.

Since intimacy is a precious gift from God, it is important that each of us evaluates how we are using it and in what context with those in our lives. Think about how you are using God's gift as you answer the following questions.

1. In your notebook or binder, make a list of the people in your life you consider to be good friends, both male and female.

2. How much time do you spend every week with each of your good friends? What sort of activities do you engage in together?

3. If you are single, are you currently dating someone? If so, how would you characterize that relationship? Are you just casually dating? Seriously dating? Ready for more commitment?

4. If you are married, think back to your courtship. Did you consider your spouse back then to be your best friend?

5. Do you now? If not, why?

6. List five characteristics you consider important in a friendship.

7. Do you have any opposite-sex platonic friendships? Have you ever considered what it would be like to be more than friends with this person?

8. Do you have a problem establishing and maintaining friendships with people of the same gender as you? If so, why do you think that is?

9. Are any of your relationships entirely online? If yes, compare those online relationships to those with your other friends. How are they different? How are they the same? Which ones do you find the most personally satisfying?

10. Do you have a personal relationship with God? Do you consider Jesus a friend?

Above all, God provides a relationship with himself to meet all of our needs, no matter how many human friendships we have or whether we are married or single. To find the ultimate in compassion, acceptance, and love, we need look no farther than Jesus. He said, "I no longer call you servants, because a servant does not know his master's business. Instead, I have called you friends, for everything that I learned from my Father I have made known to you" (John 15:15).

Helpful Resource: In our book *Hidden Dangers of the Internet,* we offer a much fuller discussion of ways unscrupulous people set up cyberspace sexual traps to ensnare unsuspecting victims. Just as we need to learn to be street-smart if we want to vacation safely in most metropolitan areas, so we need to make ourselves and our family members "Internet-smart" before we indulge in much give-and-take via our computers.

MAY GOD'S LOVE AND ACCEPTANCE *fill the voids in your life and relationships. May he give you insight into the integrity with which you should conduct your relationships. May he strengthen you to choose righteousness over duplicity in your relationships. May you choose to pursue a relationship with God over all else in your life. May you know true intimacy through Jesus.*

AFTER DAVID HAD FINISHED TALKING WITH SAUL, Jonathan became one in spirit with David, and he loved him as himself. From that day Saul kept David with him and did not let him return to his father's house. And Jonathan made a covenant with David because he loved him as himself. Jonathan took off the robe he was wearing and gave it to David, along with his tunic, and even his sword, his bow and his belt.

David hid in the field, and when the New Moon festival came, the king sat down to eat. He sat in his customary place by the wall, opposite Jonathan, but David's place was empty. Saul said nothing that day, for he thought, "Something must have happened to David to make him ceremonially unclean—surely he is unclean." But the next day, David's place was empty again. Then Saul said to his son Jonathan, "Why hasn't the son of Jesse come to the meal, either yesterday or today?"

Jonathan answered, "David earnestly asked me for permission to go to Bethlehem. He said, 'Let me go, because our family is observing a sacrifice in the town and my brother has ordered me to be there. If I have found favor in your eyes, let me go to see my brothers.' That is why he has not come to the king's table."

Saul's anger flared up at Jonathan and he said to him, "You son of a perverse and rebellious woman! Don't I know that you have sided with the son of Jesse to your own shame and to the shame of the mother who bore you? As long as the son of Jesse lives on this earth, neither you nor your kingdom will be established. Now send and bring him to me, for he must die!"

"Why should he be put to death? What has he done?" Jonathan asked his father. But Saul hurled his spear at him to kill him. Then Jonathan knew that his father intended to kill David.

In the morning Jonathan went out to the field for his meeting with David.

David got up from the south side of the stone and bowed down before Jonathan three times, with his face to the ground. Then they kissed each other and wept together—but David wept the most.

Jonathan said to David, "Go in peace, for we have sworn friendship with each other in the name of the LORD, saying, 'The LORD is witness between you and me, and between your descendants and my descendants for ever.'"

—from 1 Samuel 18 and 20

10

A friend loves at all
times, and a brother is
born for adversity.
—Proverbs 17:17

AVOID
THE TRANSFER OF INTIMACY

Maintain Successful Friendships

Angela gathered up papers, stuck them in the notebook, and made her way to the door, giving instructions and farewells as she went. To her son, she yelled down the stairs reminding him that tomorrow was garbage day and asked him to set out the recycling. Her husband got a quick peck on the cheek and a promise to be home no later than 9:30, and she added that it would be great if he could just do up those last few dishes in the sink. As she walked through the living room and out the door, Angela kept up a steady stream of words to her daughter, telling her to do her absolute best on the Spanish report due the next day and to have her dad take her to the library if she couldn't find what she needed online.

Juggling her load to open the car door, Angela jammed it all in the back, slammed the door, and climbed into the driver's seat. With a sigh, she yanked the door shut, started the engine, and pulled away from the curb. Last-minute details she should have told somebody swirled around in her head. Oh well, they'd have to do the best they could without her, at least for the next three hours.

Three hours. No laundry, no dishes, no homework...no Mom questions. No bills, no straightening, no errands...no Mom questions. Angela really looked forward to these monthly meetings of the Parks and Recreation Advisory Board. She'd first become involved when her kids had been smaller and she'd taken an active interest in the meager state of the sad equipment in several of the nearby parks. Her interest had led to her being asked by the Parks Director to sit on this committee. That was five years ago, and she now cochaired the meetings whenever he was unavailable.

Pulling into her usual parking spot, she was grateful for the ten-minute drive. Long enough to let go of the tension in the household she'd just left. Long enough to let go of the guilt she felt for leaving everyone to fend for themselves. Long enough to look forward to tackling issues she really cared about. Long enough to be pleased that her value to the committee had nothing to do with how quickly she could get dinner on the table or how white she could get socks.

As usual, Dan was pulling up at just about the same time. She really liked Dan. He'd joined the committee just after her. Funny, self-effacing, he never seemed to be without a smile. They didn't always end up on the same side of every issue, but Dan respected her point of view. While family didn't come up every time they spoke, they'd both shared tidbits about spouses, kids, and family life in general. Dan was laid back, easygoing, not only with her but with everyone on the committee.

During the last year, they'd begun to send each other messages on e-mail. It was so much easier than each of them trying to get hold of the other, even over the phone. Angela was usually busy when she was home, and Dan had three boys who seemed to live either on the phone or online. Consequently they'd given up calling and now stuck to e-mail. Dan's messages were short and to the point. Angela always attempted to keep her responses the same. Dan's time was important, and she kept the bulk of her comments restricted to park business.

Wrestling with her notebook, Angela locked up the car and joined step with Dan on the way into the meeting. They exchanged pleasantries about how the kids were doing and what their plans were going to be over the three-day weekend. Angela wasn't even into the building before something Dan said had her laughing. His humor definitely made the sometimes difficult decisions and hard work of the committee much more enjoyable.

Yes, Angela thought as Dan opened the door for her, she was glad she and Dan were friends.

SUCCESSFUL OPPOSITE-SEX FRIENDSHIPS

It is possible, of course, for men and women to engage in meaningful, satisfying friendships without their relationship taking on a sexual tone. In the previous chapter, however, we have seen some of the dangers we need to be alert to and avoid. As Scripture says, the prudent person sees danger and takes steps to avoid it (Proverbs 27:12). If they do not, Scripture goes on to say, they will suffer.

Within male-female friendships, the greatest danger to watch for is the transfer of intimacy. It leads down the path of sexualizing relationships. This is a danger whether friends are single or married. It is a danger whether the friends are Christians or non-Christians. Good, close friends of the opposite sex must always be aware that they could transfer their need for intimacy to their friend.

Staying Alert at the Wheel

Gender matters. David made Jonathan his best buddy, but he married Jonathan's sister! Pretending that gender doesn't matter ensures that, at some point, it will. It has advantages and it has risks. The advantages lie in having a relationship that will help you interact and understand the other half of the population. The risk lies in the transfer of intimacy because of the closeness of the relationship.

Maintaining a healthy male-female friendship is like driving a car. Before long a person can become quite comfortable driving. They can relax and listen to the radio, watch the sights out the window, even lean the seat back a notch. But they must never relax completely. They must never become so distracted that they take their eyes off the road. One lapse of judgment, one slip of the hand, one moment of distraction, and the car can go careening into a ditch or across several lanes of freeway traffic. The results of such a lapse can be devastating.

Yes, driving a car can be dangerous, but we still get into them every day of the week. The benefits of driving outweigh the risks, especially when our judgment and behavior can significantly cut down those risks. Because we recognize and acknowledge the risks, we make a conscious choice to do our best to operate the car responsibly.

It is the same with male-female friendships. The risk for the relationship to become sexualized, for intimacy to transfer, is always there. A prudent friend uses good judgment and upright behavior to cut down that risk significantly. A prudent friend recognizes and acknowledges the risk and makes a conscious choice at all times to conduct themselves responsibly within the friendship.

Don't Get Your Signals Crossed

In any relationship the interaction between individuals is carried out through both words and actions. It is not only what is said but also the way it is said. Nonverbal signals speak louder in relationships than the actual words themselves.

It is important, therefore, for both parties in a friendship to be aware of the signals they are sending out, both verbal and nonverbal. It does no good for the friends to say they want their relationship to remain platonic while they mindlessly engage in a high degree of physical touching and flirting. The active signals contradict and supplant the verbal message. The signals we send within a friendship must be consistent. If they are mixed, confusion can enter the friendship. Confusion becomes an open door for sin.

Wherever men and women interact, confusion seems to be a recurring theme. The basic differences in our natures, needs, and motivations require us to take special care in all our male-female interactions, whether with acquaintances, coworkers, friends, or spouses. Clarity of intentions should always be present. Even in the best circumstances, however, relational waters can get muddy in a hurry. Confusion can intrude unexpectedly, even when we think we're crystal clear about our own intentions in the friendship.

People tend to see in others and hear from others what they themselves want to see and hear. For example, one person may tell a friend about a concert she plans to attend. Her friend does not want to put down her choice of music, so he makes polite conversation about the concert, even though he has no interest in it at all. Seeing her friend's feigned interest, the woman rushes out and buys two concert tickets so they can go together. Now her friend has a dilemma. Does he go to a concert he won't like, or tell the truth and risk hurting a friend he likes? It's a simplistic example, perhaps, but such is the potential for confusion between friends.

Messages often get tangled between men and women. Not only do our signals in such friendships need to be very clear but we need to recognize that men and women will often interpret signals differently. A woman can hug another woman who is hurting without sending any kind of sexual signal. But if a woman hugs a man who is hurting, he may be apt to interpret that hug sexually. A man who listens intently to another man's woes is seen simply as a good friend, with no sexual complexity inferred. A man who listens to a woman tell her troubles may be viewed by the woman as someone who is attracted to her. Note that a physical act by a woman often may be interpreted by a man as sexual attraction, while an act of emotional connection may be interpreted by a woman as sexual attraction. The potential for confusion between men and women is rife, so our signals to one another must be exceedingly clear.

Trouble is on tap if either friend signals a willingness to cross the boundary into sexual intimacy. This boundary need not be purely physical. It is usually breached first on an emotional, verbal level. So be careful about the signals your friend perceives.

Don't Put All Your Eggs in One Basket

Platonic male-female friendships need to be limited by the recognition of gender. Such relationships are more likely to stay pure if the friends limit the number of needs each is expecting the friendship to fill. Once a solid friendship is established, each friend will naturally attempt to fill the needs they perceive in the other. A prudent friend does not ask another to fill more than is proper for the friendship. A caring friend carefully preserves the limits of the relationship to avoid causing harm for personal, selfish reasons.

These limits are especially crucial if either of the friends is married. Remember that when a person marries, they covenant with their spouse to fill intimacy needs and provide personal companionship. Even if the spouse is not filling those needs adequately, a prudent person does not expect a friendship to fill those needs. That would be a good way to hurt a friend. It would not be giving; it would be using. Using friends to gain what you lack in your marriage is self-centered and unwise.

Renter versus Owner

The transfer of intimacy in some male-female friendships occurs naturally and appropriately when the friends become spouses. (Note that we didn't say, "when the friends become lovers." Spouses first, lovers second—God's order.) If no competing relationship exists and both are single, this is often the way love works.

But, if there is a competing relationship, like a marriage, the unmarried friend must always remember that they are "renting" their friend; they do not own them. This is reciprocally true if both of the friends are married.

Let's pursue the renter/owner analogy for a moment.

If you are a renter, you need to gain permission to even occupy a house. The landlord who owns the property has the primary relationship to it. In the same way, as a friend you need to gain tacit approval of the time you occupy with your friend. Your friend's spouse has the primary relationship, and you can occupy their time and space only with that spouse's approval.

After you have gained permission to occupy the house you rented, you still cannot go around making major changes to it. Even though you live in the house, the primary relationship of the landlord is still in force. In the same way, your friendship cannot make major changes to the primary relationship in a friend's marriage. Even though you are able to spend time with your friend, their primary relationship as spouse is still in force. The more your friendship impacts the marriage, the more intrusive it becomes. A point may be reached where your bond to your friend begins to nudge your friendship into the primary relationship in your friend's life. Your friend's spouse will probably object, and rightly so.

If you are a renter, the owner has the right to inspect the premises and make themselves aware of how you are taking care of the property. In their primary role as landlord, their rights extend to overseeing your appropriate use of their property. In the same way, as a friend you need to be amenable to the desires and demands of the primary relationship. In their primary role as spouse, their rights extend to overseeing your appropriate exercise of your friendship with their mate.

If you are a renter, you need to be ready to move if the owner wants the property back. Situations change and the owner has the right to regain use of the property if and when it becomes necessary. In the same way, as a friend you need to be prepared for the primary relationship to supersede your friendship altogether. Again, situations change and the spouse has the right to regain control over the time and energy of your friend if and when it becomes necessary.

As a renter, you know all of these things. You are prepared for them because you recognize you do not own the property. You are being allowed to occupy it by permission of the owner. You understand this and accept the terms in order to rent the property.

As a friend, you need to know all of these things. You need to be prepared for them by recognizing that you do not own your friend. You are being allowed to occupy a place of friendship by permission of your friend's spouse. You must understand this and accept these terms in order to continue an appropriate friendship.

You may be having trouble equating people with property. It is not necessarily an analogy many people are comfortable with. Remember, however, that God himself establishes the concept of ownership within a marriage. "The wife's body does not belong to her alone but also to her husband," the apostle Paul wrote. "In the same way, the husband's body does not belong to him alone but also to his wife" (1 Corinthians 7:4).

Ownership in marriage comes from God. God is the ultimate landlord of all of his property, including his people. We may live in our bodies, but they belong to the Lord. He makes this quite clear in Paul's letters to the Corinthian church.

> Don't you know that you yourselves are God's temple and that God's Spirit lives in you? If anyone destroys God's temple, God will destroy him; for God's temple is sacred, and you are that temple.... Do you not know that your body is a temple of the Holy Spirit, who is in you, whom you have received from God? You are not your own; you were bought at a price. Therefore, honor God with your body. (1 Corinthians 3:16–17; 6:19–20)

God is intimately connected to us and jealously possessive of us.

He is our God and we are his people. We have been bought and paid for with blood on a cross. Exodus 34:14 says one of God's names is Jealous. When platonic male-female relationships turn sexual, the sin arouses the jealousy of both the offended spouse and God.

Acting in Safe Mode

Within a platonic male-female friendship, the possibility of slippage is always present, given the power of intimacy. In order to maintain a successful friendship, each friend must operate as a redundant, fail-safe mechanism for the other to guard against any sexualizing of the relationship.

When laboratory scientists work with complex chemical interactions, safeguards are put in place to control the results. The more complex and dangerous, the more safeguards are employed. These are called redundant, fail-safe mechanisms. The theory behind them is that if one system fails to control the chemical reaction, another backup system will take over and avert disaster. In extremely dangerous interactions such as those in a nuclear reactor, the number of redundant, fail-safe systems is staggering. The possibility of all of the systems failing simultaneously calculates to a statistical improbability.

This is how opposite-sex friends should help each other. One acts as a fail-safe to the attitude and actions of the other. If one of the friends divulges too much personal information or engages in inappropriate behavior in a moment of weakness, the other must immediately curb the interpersonal interaction to avert disaster. Each friend vows to be strong for the other. It is the least good friends can do for each other.

One of the strongest relational fail-safes is a system of faith and total trust in God. By making sure God is part of each of your male-female friendships, you add another layer of redundancy in safeguarding against accidental or planned intimacy. The indwelling of the Spirit is actually your most effective fail-safe protector. Listen to his voice to guide you in how to conduct your friendships so you can know which verbal and nonverbal signals to send and which needs you should expect the friendship to fill so that you may control the introduction of intimacy into the friendship.

SUCCESSFUL SAME-SEX FRIENDSHIPS

Dana headed to the supermarket. It was going to be a great weekend. Richard was headed out halfway across the state to help his brother lay a concrete slab behind his new house for a basketball court. He'd asked her if she wanted to come, but since Richard's brother was single, there wouldn't be anyone for her to talk to. Besides, Richard hadn't spent much time with his brother for almost a year, ever since he'd moved out there for work. They needed to be together. So she'd given her permission and blessing for him to take off work and head east to go be with his brother. Sure, they'd get the cement work done, but they'd also laugh and talk about old times. Richard would come back refreshed, happy, and grateful she'd let him go without a fuss.

Sure, she'd miss him for a few days, but she was also looking forward to his being gone. As soon as she'd heard of his plans, she called up Sue. Sue's daughter was just a few months older than Dana's son, and they'd met at church in the nursery. It wasn't long before they'd become fast friends. As soon as Sue heard that Richard was going to be out of town, she'd only wanted to know one thing: When did the snacks and videos start?

It was going to be great to devote an entire weekend to girl talk. Sue's husband was a fireman and was going to be on duty. So all plans were go. Put the kids to bed, turn down the lights, pop the popcorn into the microwave and the tape into the VCR. Dana had wanted to see the latest romantic comedy when it came out in theaters, but with the baby she'd never got around to going. Seeing it on video with Sue was the next best thing to seeing it with Richard. Of course, he probably wouldn't have wanted to see it with her even in the theater. He preferred squealing tires and exploding buildings to romantic dialogue and wistful glances. Romantic dialogue and wistful glances were right up Sue's alley. They'd munch on snacks, watch the movie, miss their husbands, and still be thankful for their time together.

So, while Richard and his brother were doing some male bonding several hundred miles away over a couple of tons of concrete, she and Sue were going to have an all-girl slumber party with two bags of popcorn and half a pound of M & M's.

She couldn't wait.

We have seen the danger that is present when people attempt to ask too much from opposite-sex friendships. Sometimes the intimacy they seek is really a desire for identification and companionship. The most obvious ways to gain these with a member of the opposite sex are through emotional and then physical union. However, identification and companionship also can be found within a same-sex friendship.

People may seek out opposites when choosing a mate, but there's something wonderful about the similarity of a same-sex friend. It is the same, easy familiarity that makes up the cohesion of a family. Instead of being part of the same family, though, the familiarity in such friendships comes from being the same gender. Some people express the concept as brotherhood or sisterhood.

Within these close relationships you have no problem with the other person misunderstanding you because of a difference in gender, no straining to understand the other person, no need for a universal translator to get your point across. Your emotional makeups sync. You mesh mentally. None of the struggles men and women often have when they are together torments same-sex friendships. Just relax and be yourself without the introduction of gender.

Looking for Love in All the Wrong Places

Some people, though, have trouble forging friendships with members of the same sex. They are much more comfortable with opposite-sex friends. It can be difficult to remain friends with those people because of the strain they place on the relationship. By limiting their relationships just to the opposite-sex kind, they ask their friends to fill both male and female roles in their lives. The broad spectrum of signals being sent in such a relationship can be extremely confusing.

We were made to be social beings. Our emotional and relational needs may be primarily filled by a small number of people, but we should enjoy the friendship of many. We have a variety of needs, and it is unrealistic to expect one person to fill all of those needs to our satisfaction. It places a tremendous burden on that person.

In a healthy marriage each spouse maintains friendships with members of their same sex. Husbands do not cut off the guys they know. The time and energy they have to maintain the friendships may change, but most men will continue to invest in male friendships after marriage. Wives do not say good-bye to all of their girlfriends at the altar. A wife will still spend time visiting with and talking to her girlfriends long after she is married. The amount of time she is able to spend with them will diminish, but smart ladies will still find time to be together.

Marking Territory

Why would anybody shun same-sex friendships? It's neither normal or natural to do so. People who do may look upon others of their sex as competitors. If they constantly compare themselves to others of their same sex and feel a sense of competition, the potential of a friendship with someone who is either more attractive, stronger, or more competent than they feel they are is remote.

People who have trouble engaging in same-sex friendships also tend to view members of the opposite sex in strictly sexualized terms. In other words, people of the opposite sex are potential targets for sexual conquest and people of the same sex are potential rivals in that conquest.

These people operate very much like male territorial wolves, regardless of their sex. For these male wolves, all of the female wolves within their marked territory are considered possible breeders. The wolf will not allow other males within the territory. He is ever on guard, vigilant against competition from another male wolf. Instead of associating with other male wolves, he is a loner. When he interacts with other males, it is for the purpose of establishing dominance. When he interacts with females, it is for the purpose of breeding or ensuring the females' continued presence within his sphere of influence.

Whether male or female, these people view themselves and others through the lens of sexualization. They cannot become friends with someone of the same sex because they are always on guard for possible competition from their own kind. They also have trouble establishing and maintaining opposite-sex friendships without attempting to interject sexualization into the relationship.

If these people are male, the overriding problem is lust. Their lust fuels their obsession with women as sexual objects to either be conquered or controlled within their spheres of influence. Therefore, other men set off their territorial alarm. Men cannot be their friends for they see other men as invaders of their territory.

If these people are female, the overriding problem is power and, ultimately, control. Their need for control fuels their obsession to manipulate the men around them through their sexuality. They view other women as threats to their control over the men around them. The presence and influence of other women sets up a jamming field through which their sexuality must penetrate and dominate. Other women are not considered friends because their very presence destabilizes such women's control over their environment.

Whether male or female, the primary need of such people is control, not friendship. The only same-sex friendships they have will be ones they feel they can control. The man may choose to be friends with another man, but only with one who is not perceived as a sexual threat. The reason for the friendship may be to either talk about women or to gain assistance in obtaining women. A beautiful but insecure woman may choose to be a friend with another woman only after she is assured that the other woman presents no threat to her sexual sphere. The reason for the friendship may be to present herself as physically superior in comparison or to assist in her obsession to control those around her.

These are not successful same-sex friendships. Control should never be the theme for friends. Competition should never thwart friendships.

Avoid the Wolves

To have successful, same-sex friendships, then, you need to avoid people like these. You may unknowingly enter into a friendship with one of them, but their actions will make it impossible for you to maintain any sort of lasting friendship. Remember, they aren't really interested in being your friend. What they want is your assistance, compliance, and acceptance of their control.

If you run into a person like this, protect yourself and withdraw from the relationship. Plenty of people of your gender in this world earnestly desire to have a same-sex friend. Keep looking.

God knows we need deep, same-sex friendships to fill our lives with meaning and purpose. He provided two such examples within his word. In the Book of Ruth, we learn of the deep, committed friendship of two women, Naomi and Ruth. This friendship bore the brunt of hardship, death, travel, and even remarriage. The bond of these two women remained strong through it all. Some of the most beautiful words portraying the strength of friendship come from this book. "Don't urge me to leave you or to turn back from you," Ruth told Naomi. "Where you go I will go, and where you stay I will stay. Your people will be my people and your God my God" (Ruth 1:16).

The friendship between David and Jonathan was so deep that it encompassed even their souls. "After David has finished talking with Saul, Jonathan became one in spirit with David, and he loved him as himself" (1 Samuel 18:1).

Having successful, satisfying same-sex friendships can provide emotional support. They allow each friend to meet needs within the context of the friendship. C. S. Lewis was right when he said in *The Four Loves* that same-sex friendships are the most comfortable relationships on earth. They provide a safe, relaxing friendship without the added stress of sexual tension.

———— Fuel for Thought ————

Friendships are necessary for emotional health. Even Jesus, who maintained continual contact with God, his heavenly Father, had good, dear friends in this life, both male and female. Anyone who reads the New Testament can see the love Jesus had for other men, such as his disciples, and for the women who accompanied him, such as Mary and Martha. Good friends of both genders add to our quality of life and allow us to enjoy sweet fellowship.

1. Review the following list of ways to maintain successful male-female relationships.

- Recognize gender and accept it as a limiting factor.

- Keep your signals consistent and platonic.

- Don't ask for more than you should out of the friendship.

- Accept and adjust for your friend's primary relationships.

- Be strong for your friend in case he or she slips.

- Look to God for guidance in your friendship.

2. Think about the male-female friendships you have now. In your notebook or binder, write how you are doing in each of the above areas. As you review male-female friendships in your past, is there some area you seem to have perpetual trouble with? Which one is it? Why do you think you have trouble with this area?

3. In order to have healthy opposite-sex friendships, it is necessary to have healthy same-sex friendships. Review the following aspects of same-sex friendships. Do any of them stand out to you? Have you had trouble enjoying same-sex friendships in the past?

   a. Do you view other members of the same sex as sexual competition?

   b. As you look over your same-sex friendships, have you ever had the kind of soul-bonded relationship as exhibited by Jonathan and David in Scripture? If not, can you visualize yourself in such a relationship?

   c. Do you tend to view the value of a friendship for what it can do for you as opposed to what you can give to the friendship?

   d. If you are a woman, write down how women generally respond to you. Write down how men generally respond to you.

   e. If you are a man, write down how other men interact with you. Write down how women respond to you.

   f. Have you ever used a same-sex friendship as a way to manipulate how you feel about yourself?

4. If you have realized an inability on your part to initiate or maintain same-sex friendships, ask yourself the following additional questions:

a. Do you enjoy the sexual attraction of members of the opposite sex? Do you use it as a way to gain compliance or control over others?

b. When you come into contact with a member of the opposite sex, is your first inclination to respond to them in a sexual way?

c. When you come into contact with a member of the same sex, is your first inclination to compare yourself to them?

d. What is your response if you find them lacking?

e. What is your response if you find yourself lacking?

f. When you were growing up, did you enjoy a better relationship with your father or your mother?

g. As an adult, do you have a better relationship now with your father or with your mother?

We are complex creatures. Our needs are varied. It usually takes more than one person to meet those needs. Even God presents himself to us in three separate personalities. It would be an error for us to think a single human being will be able to meet our every need. Seek out friendships with men and women both to fill your own needs and to work toward filling the needs of others. We need each other as friends.

Helpful Resource: In their fine book *Relationships,* published by Zondervan, Drs. Les and Leslie Parrott explore the blessings all of us can unlock by learning to cultivate healthy same-sex friendships.

MAY GOD BLESS YOUR SEARCH *for good and true friends in this life. May he enable you to be a good, true friend to others. May his Spirit befriend you in those times when your human relationships fail. May he gently use the friends in your life to bring you closer to him.*

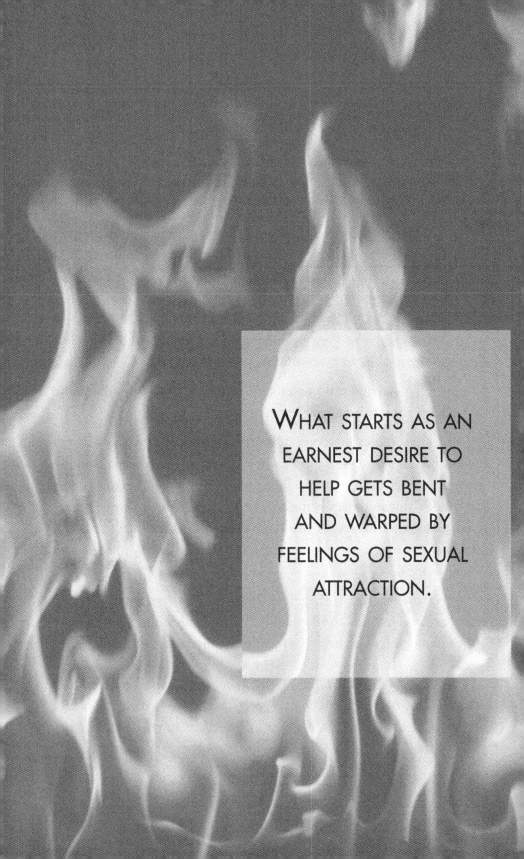

WHAT STARTS AS AN
EARNEST DESIRE TO
HELP GETS BENT
AND WARPED BY
FEELINGS OF SEXUAL
ATTRACTION.

11

The body is not meant for sexual immorality, but for the Lord.... Flee from sexual immorality.
—1 Corinthians 6:13, 18

RECOGNIZE

A COUNSELING CONFLICT

Compassion Can Lead to Passion

She came through the door a broken woman. Hope was hanging by the thinnest thread. Her life was in shambles. Her self-esteem had sunk so low she couldn't even find it to lift it up. She was dying, and he was her only hope. Please, she begged him with her eyes. She'd do anything he said if he'd just take her pain away.

Her cries for help caught him like a wave. Usually he could detach himself from the suffering of his clients, knowing he would be able to help. She was different. Her look of total dependence, trust, and submission overwhelmed him. Her very life was dependent upon his ability to help her. She trusted him completely to know what to do. She submitted herself wholly to his control. Together they were like strands of a cord. He was tied to her.

As he sat and listened to her story of abandonment, manipulation, and verbal abuse, he could barely contain his fury. This woman's husband had treated her abysmally. Yet somehow she was trying to repair the relationship. She was concerned about herself, but more than anything, she wanted her husband to be the man she knew he could be.

Could he, would he, help? She'd wanted to know.

How could he not?

Over the course of the next several months, she opened up her life to him like the pages of a book. With quiet detachment she wove a story of personal debasement. Her husband, he concluded to himself, had no concept of tenderness or compassion. Her only value to him, it seemed, was as a possession. She was his wife, and he had no intention of letting her go. He also had no intention of truly loving her. His definition of husband and wife was a warped image of domination and callous disregard. It amazed him week after week that she hadn't been totally crushed by the experience.

Her only act of defiance to her husband was in seeing him. She told him in a wavering voice what would happen to her if her husband ever found out she was seeing a marriage counselor. They had to keep it secret. She was siphoning off funds from household accounts to be able to afford his fees.

Usually, he made it a habit to tell his wife what was going on at work. He was careful not to betray confidences, but he would flesh out for her, in general terms, the kinds of problems he was seeing. It had always been nice to have a sounding board and someone to vent his frustrations to over the utter stupidity of some people. His wife was sympathetic and often provided him with a different point of view, which had proved extremely helpful in the past.

This time, however, every time he started to talk to his wife about this client, he would stop and change the subject. For some reason he was concerned about the tone of his voice or the expression in his face if he talked about her to his wife. She was perceptive, being married to a counselor. He was afraid she'd pick up on his confused feelings about his client. It didn't dawn on him until later that both he and his client were keeping their relationship secret from their spouses.

More than once, he'd counseled her to leave the bum. That was when her strength finally showed through. No, she'd insisted. Divorce was not an option for her. She'd made her choice and was going to stick with it. Besides, he hadn't always been so cruel to her. Why, when they'd been dating, he'd been absolutely charming. He was so attentive and sweet. She just knew, if she could keep herself together, he could be that way again. His life was just stressful right now. All he needed was a little time. She didn't need anyone's help to leave her husband. She needed his help to be strong enough to stay.

Part of him knew he should have counseled her to look for someone else's help at that point. His best advice was to leave the bum and sue him for every cent he had. But he couldn't bring himself to turn her over to somebody else. Heaven knows she'd been abused by her husband; he couldn't bear the thought of her being improperly counseled by another therapist. His best course of action, he decided, was to try to convince her how terrible her husband really was and how unlikely it was that he would ever change.

She had married him young, not even out of her teens. He'd seen her picture in the local photography studio in the small town where the two of them had lived. It was her senior picture from high school. The photographer had been so taken with her that he'd asked if he could put her picture up to promote his business. She'd been flattered and agreed. Little did she know it would interest not only potential clients for the photographer but also a man eight years older who, upon seeing the picture, vowed that girl would be his wife.

Ten years later, the counselor could still see the beautiful, innocent girl obscured by a decade of a terrible marriage. Her form, though painfully thin, still bore the evidence of its former, voluptuous nature. More and more, he found himself wondering what she'd look like if she could relax enough to eat a little more, if she would just cut her hair a different way or wear a little more makeup. Her face was always so pale.

To his surprise, one day she showed up with a new haircut. Her husband had been enraged and told her she looked like a man with her hair cut short like that. It was really cute, though, and made her look several years younger. He complimented her on the cut. She shyly admitted she'd done it because she thought he'd like it.

He playfully reached out to run his hands over her hair. The look she gave him took his breath away. With a shock he realized how receptive she was to the smallest gesture of kindness. Without thinking he let his hand work its way down her hair and across the warm curve of her cheek and chin. Eyes wide open, she tipped her head up in response to his touch, bringing her face closer to his.

With a catch in his throat, he told her she was beautiful and no one had the right to treat her so badly. Her eyes reached out and anchored him to her with a look of trusting surrender. Nothing was left to think about except the feel of her lips on his.

The overwhelming majority of counseling situations are accomplished without becoming sexualized. For the small percentage that do, the majority are female clients becoming sexually involved with male professionals. This is a breach of both professional and personal conduct.

Very rarely the professional involved is a sexual predator or manipulator who uses his business as a platform for satisfying his sexual desires and need for control. Fortunately, the aggressive behavior of this type eventually catches up to him professionally, legally, and personally. Unfortunately, he may have sexualized several client relationships before his behavior is exposed and addressed.

More frequently when a professional-client relationship becomes sexualized, it is done from a platform of good intentions. What starts as an earnest desire to help gets bent and warped by feelings of sexual attraction. The professional really does want to respond to the needs of his client, but he chooses an inappropriately sexualized way to do so.

If you are a professional counselor, you hold a position of great trust in the lives of those you help. Often they are desperate and look to you to rescue them from unbearable situations. The trust they place in you translates into a high degree of power over them. They literally put themselves in your hands. For this reason, your conduct must be professional and aboveboard at all times. At no moment can you relax your professional, personal, and/or spiritual standards.

Remember, your control of the counseling situation can tempt you to exert inappropriate power over the direction the relationship takes. Avoid using this power to alter the parameters of your relationship with the other person for your own personal or sexual benefit. No matter how compelling it may seem, what they need from you most is professional guidance, not personal engagement.

WHEN FORCES ALIGN

People who enter a healing profession, be they doctors, lawyers, counselors, or therapists, need to be aware of the potent combination of forces that coalesce within a counseling situation. We have talked before about the power of partnering in relationships. We have spoken about the compelling nature of caring and sharing. We have seen the danger inherent when a relationship involves an element of unequal power. All of these components are present in a counseling situation.

Professionals and clients partner to solve a problem. Their partnering requires trust and a high degree of openness and honesty. In some situations, the "us versus them" mind-set prevalent in all partnering turns out to be literally the truth, especially if an element of abuse colors the client's past or present.

The amount of work both sides invest is often considerable and can last for months or even years. Together, client and counselor work as a team, sometimes facing crises that intensify the sense of togetherness against all odds. Each partner must trust the other either to dispense needed advice or to carry out that advice. Their counseling relationship bonds them together.

The healing professions naturally attract people who have a highly developed capacity for compassion and caring. They tend to be empathetic and sympathetic. These caring people have an understanding of human pain and a determined desire to alleviate that pain. They are willing to sacrifice time and energy to fill the needs they perceive in others. For many, it is their business, yes, but it is also their mission in life.

The client often shares revealing and highly personal information with the professional. The greater the crisis, the more necessary it is to delve deep inside the mind of the person to find the answers they need to resolve their situation.

The professional cares about the life and health of the client, and this caring is a vital component of the trust necessary in counseling situations. A troubled client may be extremely vulnerable and need assurance that the professional generally cares before exposing sensitive secrets.

People in trouble are vulnerable. They often do not have the necessary expertise to extricate themselves from their trouble or to find a way to cope with their problem, so they turn to professionals for help. They voluntarily place themselves in a subordinate position to the professional in order to gain help. The professional, of necessity, takes the lead in searching for a solution to the problem, assuming a dominant position, and the client, a subordinate one, for the length of the counseling.

So partnering, compassion, and position—along with the inherent dangers of each—are present in a counseling situation. All of the volatility we've seen in these factors now combines in a single relationship. No wonder these relationships sometimes become inappropriately sexualized. They are minefields waiting for one mistaken step.

He felt sick. He couldn't believe it had gone this far. What started out as a gentle touch on the cheek ended forty-five minutes later with his professional and marital obligations completely disregarded. All that had mattered during that time was the two of them together.

He had deluded himself into thinking he could stop it before it got this far. Now he realized that he hadn't really wanted it to stop.

He had tried to rationalize it by saying he was just giving her an example of how it was supposed to be, so she'd know that what her husband was giving her was wrong. Now he was the one in the wrong, but it didn't feel that way.

He had blinded himself by saying it would only be this once, that it didn't need to go any farther. Now he saw how much he wanted it to continue.

She was like a different woman, kissing him and telling him she wouldn't tell anyone. Her face was animated and intense. She promised to protect him. She certainly didn't want her husband to know. There was really no need for him to tell his wife. After all, he was helping her. She knew he could get in trouble, and she was effusively grateful for his concern for her. She'd never realized it could be this way.

It was their secret—just, could they, please, do it again next week?

At this point he should have done a lot of things. He didn't do any of them. What he did was hold her close and promise they would.

INFORMAL COUNSELING

Some of you may be saying, "This chapter doesn't apply to me. I'm not a professional counselor, therapist, doctor, or attorney. My job doesn't put me in a position of offering advice or counseling other people. So this isn't something I have to worry about, right?"

Not necessarily.

The potential for a counseling situation to become sexualized is not just present for professionals. The danger exists anytime two people enter into even informal counseling. Informal counseling is any situation where one person goes to another for advice and help. The potent combination of partnering, compassion, and position still are in force, though in varying degrees depending upon the situation. Nonetheless, they are present and cannot be dismissed as having no effect.

If a man goes to a woman he knows for advice and counsel, it is probably for a personal problem, not a work-related one. Most men either keep their own counsel on work-related problems or ask another man. But if the problem is personal or if it involves a misunderstanding with a woman, a man may seek out a female to find help. The compassion index in a situation like this is high. Flattered that the man has come to her, the woman may do everything she can think of to help him.

The man may not feel comfortable showing his confusion or hurt to others about the situation for which he needs advice. However, if he feels comfortable enough with this particular woman to turn to her for help, he will be more inclined to show the depth of his feelings. His emotional outpouring can trigger even greater feelings of compassion on the part of his woman advisor.

If a woman goes to a man for advice, on the other hand, it need not be over something personal. It could be about work or life in general. Women are used to seeking advice from other women on a whole gamut of problems. If a woman does go to a man for advice, he likely will be someone she admires, someone she believes to have the knowledge or expertise to help her with her problem. In this situation the position index is high.

This disparity of position may cause the man to develop feelings of protection for the woman. In coming to him for advice, she may appear to be asking for protection as well as assistance. His response may be to view himself in the role of a knight in shining armor, protecting a damsel in distress. Of course, in most of the knight-dragon tales you may recall that after the knight has saved the damsel, she becomes his lover. In this situation, fact has a tendency to imitate fiction.

If the man and the woman know each other very well, raise the needle for the partnering index. Their ease with each other removes many normal inhibitions, even in a counseling situation. Because the two know each other and may be fully aware of the situation involved, they have a heightened tendency to intensify the "us versus them" mentality. We have already seen where that road can lead. If one of the two has entertained thoughts or fantasies about the other, an informal counseling situation can easily propel those thoughts into actions.

WOLVES IN SHEEP'S CLOTHING

All of us know that some professionals are sexual predators who use their position to prey on vulnerable people. Thankfully, these situations are rare and they almost always come to light. More insidious are the opportunists who manipulate informal counseling situations for their own ends. They can be either the seeker or the provider of the informal counseling. Watch out for them whenever you seek the help of someone else or when somebody comes to you for advice.

These sexual opportunists are aware of the power of situations that involve partnering, sharing, and position. They are also aware that crisis situations can cause people to disconnect from their normal friendship and sexual boundaries. Opportunists of this kind will often exploit these conditions for personal reasons.

RUN, DON'T WALK

Whether the counseling situation is a professional one or an informal one, it is vital to recognize its potential to become sexualized. A degree in a fancy wooden frame, hanging prominently on a wall, does not insulate the expert from slipping in their professional and personal conduct. The informal, casual give-and-take of a non-professional situation does not remove any of the components that can contribute to a sexualized relationship. Wisdom in dealing with both is essential.

All of the components that can lead to a sexualized counseling relationship are given by God. We are allowed to partner with him as he works in this world. He is the Father of compassion and caring. His word outlines hierarchies for both family and work situations, firmly establishing the principle of position. None of these elements is intrinsically sinful.

God has given us each other, family, and the church to meet our needs. He encourages us to confess our sins to one another, to go to each other for help and advice in times of crisis. Acknowledging that you need help for a problem is not wrong. Accepting the responsibility of entering into the life and thoughts of someone else to offer advice and counsel is not wrong. Each of these instances, in and of itself, is not sinful.

But in high-voltage counseling situations, we tread a fine line between doing good and doing evil. We may start out desiring to do good and end up simply desiring. Only by acknowledging the danger can we keep from sin. When sin presents itself as a temptation to sexual immorality, Scripture says we must flee. Not walk. Not stroll. Not amble out of its path. We are to run, to flee. Sin and sexual desire are powerful forces. When the two are combined, we must flee before we become ensnared.

——— Fuel for Thought ———

Often we get into trouble in counseling situations because we either fail to notice the signs of the situation becoming sexualized or we ourselves give off signals of an openness that allow the situation to become sexualized. Consider how you have dealt with situations like these in the past.

1. Have you ever sought out a counselor? Was this person a professional, or was it someone other than a professional?

2. Why did you choose to seek out this person? What did you hope to gain from the relationship?

3. Have you ever been sought out for advice and counsel? Are you a professional counselor, therapist, doctor, or attorney?

4. Why do you believe you were chosen by the person needing your help? What did they wish to gain?

5. Was there a time during the course of the relationship when you felt your attitude toward that person changing?

6. Was there a time during the course of the relationship when you felt the attitude of the other person changing?

7. Does being in a position of dominance over someone give you a sense of satisfaction? Is this sense of satisfaction ever sexual?

8. Does being in a position of needing someone give you a sense of satisfaction? Is this sense of satisfaction ever sexual?

MAY THE SPIRIT OF GOD, *the Comforter and Counselor, guide you in all of your counseling situations, whether you are a seeker or a provider. May you flee from immorality in all of its forms. May you draw near to God.*

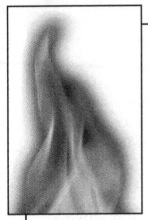

SAMSON FELL IN LOVE WITH DELILAH. The Philistines went to her and said, "See if you can lure him into showing you the secret of his great strength and how we can overpower him so that we may tie him up and subdue him. Each one of us will give you eleven hundred shekels of silver."

So Delilah said to Samson, "Tell me the secret of your great strength and how you can be tied up and subdued."

"If anyone ties me with seven fresh thongs that have not been dried, I'll become as weak as any other man."

Then the rulers of the Philistines brought her seven fresh thongs that had not been dried, and she tied him with them. With men hidden in the room, she called, "Samson, the Philistines are upon you!" But he snapped the thongs as easily as a piece of string snaps when it comes close to a flame.

Then Delilah said to Samson, "You have made a fool of me; you lied to me. Come now, tell me how you can be tied."

"If anyone ties me securely with new ropes that have never been used, I'll become as weak as any other man."

So Delilah took new ropes and tied him with them. Then, with men hidden in the room, she called, "Samson, the Philistines are upon you!" But he snapped the ropes off his arms as if they were threads.

Then she said to him, "How can you say, 'I love you,' when you won't confide in me?" With such nagging she prodded him day after day until he was tired to death.

So he told her everything. "No razor has ever been used on my head, because I have been a Nazirite set apart to God since birth. If my head were shaved, my strength would leave me, and I would become as weak as any other man."

When Delilah saw that he had told her everything, she sent word to the Philistines, "Come back once more; he has told me everything." Having put him to sleep on her lap, she called a man to shave off his hair, and so began to subdue him. And his strength left him.

Then she called, "Samson, the Philistines are upon you!"

He awoke from his sleep and thought, "I'll go out as before and shake myself free." But he did not know that the LORD had left him.

Then the Philistines seized him, gouged out his eyes and took him down to Gaza. Binding him with bronze shackles, they set him to grinding in the prison.

—from Judges 16

12

If someone is caught in a sin, you who are spiritual should restore him gently. But watch yourself, or you also may be tempted.
—Galatians 6:1–2

AVOID
THE SMOLDERING COUCH

Share Thoughts, Not Intimacy

Just as he was headed out the front door, the phone rang. The receptionist had already gone home, naturally. Within the span of three rings, a battle raged: to pick it up or not to pick it up. That was the question. It was late, but what if the call was important? The machine could pick it up, but why not just see who it was? He reached the phone as it was beginning its fourth ring.

The moment he heard the voice on the other end, his jaw clenched. Patience, he counseled himself. Just hear her out; sometimes, that was all it took. For the next several minutes the most he could respond with was an occasional grunt or monosyllabic answer. When she finally began to run down, he seized the opportunity to take control of the conversation. She needed to calm down, he told her. Surely it wasn't as bad as she was making it out to be. Looking up at the clock, he fleetingly wished he'd let the phone ring.

No, he repeated, he wasn't perturbed that she'd called. He understood she was upset, but she really did need to get control of herself. Her appointment was in three days, and from what she'd told him, the situation could wait until then. No, the place was closed, and policy was to conduct sessions during office hours only. Surely she could see the wisdom in that.

Yes, he understood she trusted him, but that wasn't the point. The office had rules, and he agreed with them. No after-hours sessions when nobody else was in the office. Of course, he could call Suzie and see if she would meet the two of them tomorrow evening...oh, that wouldn't work. Okay, well, could she wait, then, until her regularly scheduled appointment? Good. He'd see her then.

With a sigh, he cradled the receiver. *Why him?* he thought as he finished locking up. Why couldn't she have found someone else to go to? He could always fake some sort of obscure malady or unscheduled emergency and pass her off to another therapist. No, that wouldn't be right.

And besides, her behavior was just an indication of how confused she was. He knew her continual attempts to introduce a sexual component into their relationship was another cry for help. Just as he knew he could help her, if he had the patience. Once he wore down her insistence on introducing sex every time they got together, the truth of her situation could come out. She really did want help, but she was afraid to trust him without the component of sex. She was using sex to try to control him so she could control her own therapy. She also used it as a cover for the pain in her life. But now the pain was coming through no matter what she did.

From what she'd already shared with him, he could see that this was a consistent pattern in her relationships with men. She didn't trust them unless she was sleeping with them, and even then she still didn't really trust them.

Yes, he could help her. It would take all of his professional skills to break through her wall of denial and all of his personal patience to work with such a difficult client. It certainly would take all of his procedural policies to buffer himself against the onslaught of her sexuality.

She was, after all, an extremely attractive woman.

PROFESSIONAL RISK ASSESSMENT

Partnering, caring, and position. We have seen repeatedly how these components pose a risk of sexualization. Anytime a man and a woman are involved in a counseling situation these risk factors are present. But life is not without risk. If we tried to remove risk in our lives, we would end up in the equivalent of a hermetically sealed bubble, and life would cease to be life. In the face of any danger, you and I have to ask, "Is the risk worth taking?"

If you are a professional counselor, therapist, doctor, or attorney, you will probably have a different answer than someone engaged in an informal counseling situation. For you that risk is part of your job. People are risky, but people are clients. No risk equals no clients, which equals no livelihood. In order to conduct your business, you must take risks. In order to survive in your business, you need to learn to minimize those risks. God commands, "Do not withhold good from those who deserve it, when it is in your power to act" (Proverbs 3:27), but he doesn't intend for us to destroy ourselves in the process.

The Value of Saying No

One of the most important and fundamental ways you can avoid a sexualized relationship within a professional setting is to refuse to do business with some individuals. The almost automatic assumption that anyone who walks through your doors should become your client is false. The money you make by dealing with certain individuals simply may not be worth the risk.

If you feel a persistent, sexual attraction to a client, turn that client over to someone else. Find an associate to handle the situation.

Your ego may keep saying you can weather your attraction and keep the relationship professional, but the deeper the professional relationship grows, the greater the pull of your sexual attraction likely will become. Remember, sexual attraction fueled by lust can be intoxicating. It may cloud your professional judgment before you know it. You may keep your conversations completely professional, but your client still may pick up nonverbal evidence of your attraction. For your sake, and for your client's sake, don't play with fire. The earlier you transfer your client to someone else you trust, the better it will be for both of you.

Some clients may be used to dealing with members of the opposite sex consistently through a sexual lens. This may be a comfort issue for them. This is how they have learned to deal with the world. If so, it might be prudent to at least suggest their going to a same-sex professional in order to minimize complications to their situation. Beware, also, of taking on a sexual manipulator or climber as a client. You may have every intention of keeping the relationship professional, but they always have a different agenda. Their continual introduction of a sexual component into your relationship may not be a comfort issue as much as a control issue. By sending them to a same-sex professional you remove an area of control. This could be exactly what they need to be able to accept the counsel their situation requires.

The first line of defense for avoiding an inappropriately sexualized professional relationship is to get out and stay out of that relationship.

It's Not What You Know but Who You Know

Networking within your profession makes you and your colleagues safer and more effective. If it becomes necessary for you to terminate a professional relationship, for example, you will at least be able to recommend a replacement. If you are referring a sexual manipulator or climber, however, you should inform your associate or colleague of that individual's propensity and give them the opportunity to decline to involve themselves in that client's situation. A network of professionals can offer you forewarning of a potential problem client, professional accountability, and a pool of people you can go to for help or supervision when you encounter a problem client or situation.

Whatever helping profession you are in, spend some time getting to know your colleagues both near and far. Smart referrals require that you know who is competent and professional and who's not.

The Power of Three

Once you accept someone as a client and begin a professional relationship, factor in an air of accountability for your actions. Your actions should always be characterized by openness, as opposed to secrecy. Whenever possible, conduct your professional relationship in the open.

This does not mean you must always have an open door. Naturally, most counseling situations involve the exchange of privileged information. It may not be possible or advisable either to have the door to your office open or to have a third person present. However, you should have other people in the vicinity who know who you are meeting with.

Even if only the two of you are physically present in your office, never forget that a third Presence is there. Nothing is secret to God. He is aware of you and your actions at all times, whether you are conducting personal or professional business. You are never truly alone. Every deed, every action, is seen by God. He expects you to maintain integrity in all areas of your life. Remember his admonition in Colossians 3:17 to do everything in word or deed in the name of the Lord.

Use the presence and power of three to remind you of the accountability you have to yourself, your client, and your God.

Obey the Rules

Once you agree to a professional relationship with a client and are pursuing that relationship, don't let familiarity breed contempt for professional rules of conduct. If your profession has specific rules regarding clients, don't take shortcuts. Maintain those rules. Over the span of years those rules have come about, probably, through the mistakes and missteps of others. The rules may seem cumbersome, even awkward, but consistency in keeping them will help you steer the relationship away from dangerous shoals. Once you make an exception, the next time becomes that much easier.

All of us who are licensed, well-trained professionals spent long years in school learning the skills we use to help people. Our studies should have included courses on the ethical standards for our vocation. If you are unfamiliar with the rules of conduct and ethics for your particular profession, contact the professional organization that oversees your field. Counselors, therapists, doctors, and attorneys all have professional organizations that have rules of conduct and ethics guiding their members' behavior. If you don't know what they are, find out.

Everything in Its Place

Business should be conducted at places of business. Your office is your professional zone. It is the place where your acknowledgment of the rules of your profession can be greatest. Your desk, your receptionist, your degrees, your family pictures, even your front door—all are reminders of what should be the proper parameters of your relationships. They are buffers that remind you of your responsibilities not to allow a relationship to become inappropriately sexual.

Situations may arise during the course of business, however, that require you to practice your profession at some other location. Care and wisdom should dictate acceptable and unacceptable location alternatives. If another location is necessary, it should be a public venue, not a private one.

Do Not Date Clients

If you are single, the next client who walks through your door could be the love of your life. Hard to know. This much you can know: that you should never mix a personal and business relationship. If it becomes obvious that you wish to pursue a personal relationship with a client or with the professional who is counseling you, terminate your professional relationship first. At the first realization of how you are really feeling about the other person, you need to tell them. This is the only honest thing to do. Your honesty will allow them to decide what action they want to take in response to your feelings about them.

While it may seem like a natural fit—to say nothing of a time-saver—to try to maintain a professional and personal relationship with someone, the one compromises and complicates the other. Decide which relationship should take precedence and act accordingly. If a personal relationship is possible and desired, terminating the professional one should be no problem.

Pride Goes before a Fall

As he listened to her talk, he couldn't keep from observing her body language. She always seemed to sit sideways in the chair, allowing her already short skirt to ride up her thigh. Feigning a look of nonchalance, her right index finger kept moving back and forth across the edge of her skirt hem, just to make sure he didn't miss seeing her legs.

Whenever she spoke, she tended to affect a whispered response. Invariably, he had to lean forward to hear her. Her clothing was never overtly sexualized, more in an understated way. Her blouse wasn't low cut, but by unbuttoning just one more button, the swell of her breasts was clearly visible.

This wasn't working, he had to admit to himself. He thought he'd be able to break through her obsessive need to introduce a sexual component during counseling. He thought his total unresponsiveness to her subtle sexualizations would act as a therapeutic cold shower. It had been going on for several months, though, and she was showing no signs of cooling off. He had no intention of waiting any further.

Honesty forced him to admit that he wasn't going to be the one to help her. It would be better for her if she would go to a female counselor. He wasn't at all sure how she'd take his suggestion, but he knew it was time to make it. Ultimately, he had to consider what would be in her best interest. Her interest in him was getting in the way of his ability to help. Nothing else could be done.

She wasn't cooling off, and he didn't want to risk heating up.

One line of defense in any relationship that has the potential to become sexualized is to recognize that potential. Be alert to the possibility of temptation entering your professional life. Don't make the mistake of compartmentalizing yourself into private and professional areas, thinking that God only has a part in your private life while you are quite capable of handling your professional life all by yourself. Your entire life belongs to God as a witness to his power and glory. Sin is not choosy. It will use whatever area it can—professional or private—to cause you to fall.

No part of your life is private to God, of course. No segment of your life escapes his awareness. No aspect of your life is exempt from his rules. You are accountable for all of it.

Some have the warped idea that business is somehow exempt from Christian principles. Erroneously they rationalize that their spiritual life is private and disconnected from the world of business. This allows them to pick up God, along with their Bibles, on the way out the door Sunday morning and, inversely, to leave God lying on the hall table as they leave for work on Monday. Such thinking is foolishness. God is in control of all aspects of our lives, even the business you call "yours."

"Now listen, you who say, 'Today or tomorrow we will go to this or that city, spend a year there, carry on business and make money.' Why, you do not even know what will happen tomorrow.... Instead, you ought to say, 'If it is the Lord's will, we will live and do this or that'" (James 4:13–15).

So conduct your business with eyes open, aware that God is watching, aware of the potential for a professional relationship to become inappropriately sexualized. Don't join your colleagues who have ruined their reputations and careers by underestimating the seductive power of transference between professionals and those they seek to help. Is anyone more pitiful than a professional with highly acclaimed skills—a doctor, a pastor, an attorney, a licensed counselor—who is legally barred from using those skills because of unfortunate sexual improprieties with clients? These fallen giants are not unlike ancient Samson, once so honored because of the extraordinary powers God had given him, once a hero God used to help the helpless, but in the end a blind, helpless, humiliated weakling, disqualified when he misjudged the power of sex to cost him his power. Be on the lookout for anything that could cause you to stumble and fall. Don't imagine that you are exempt. "Pride goes before destruction, a haughty spirit before a fall" (Proverbs 16:18).

Inappropriate Gratitude

It is almost a cliché for patients to fall in love with their doctors. An overwhelming sense of gratitude rises when someone has helped us with a difficult situation. During times of difficulty or crisis, a person may misinterpret these feelings of gratitude as feelings of love. The dependency the person in crisis has on the professional can be already extremely strong. This dependency can also be interpreted as a need for a personal, even a sexual relationship. Deluded by the strong but misleading feelings, the client may decide they cannot live without this person who has so helped them, to whom they are so indebted.

Awareness of this phenomenon should motivate the professional to keep all conversations and actions completely aboveboard and beyond reproach. Any ambiguous conversation or ambivalent action could be misinterpreted by a client who has a tendency to romanticize their relationship with a professional. Clarity at all times by the professional should help to cut down on the miscues and misunderstandings inherent in this phenomenon.

If as a professional you are being tempted or if you find yourself currently involved in an inappropriately sexualized relationship, you need to seek help and guidance to stop. Your own pride and denial mechanisms will be working overtime to try to rationalize your situation. Right now you need to take these three steps:

1. *Review the ethical guidelines* of your profession and use them honestly to assess your current relationship.

2. *Seek peer support* from others in your profession to help you withstand the pressures of your own sexual desires.

3. *Seek counsel* from an expert in dealing with issues of this kind. Consider calling our Center at 1-888-771-5166.

Whatever you do, do not either give in to the temptation of a sexualized client relationship or continue with a sexualized client relationship.

INFORMAL RISK ASSESSMENT

Risk also needs to be assessed in informal counseling situations. No professional onus pushes you to engage in or continue with an informal counseling situation, but you probably feel a personal one. People generally tend to go to family, friends, or acquaintances for help. We feel duty-bound to assist them.

Head Up—Eyes Forward

Be extra careful if you find yourself giving advice or counsel to someone of the opposite sex. If both of you are single, the potential for this situation to become sexualized is high. If you feel comfortable enough to enter into even an informal counseling situation, you risk a transfer of intimacy. Lacking professional training, you may fail to see the signs of danger in time to avert disaster.

If one of you is married, you should seriously consider avoiding any informal counseling situation that would involve discussion of intimate or personal information. Your relationship is simply not an appropriate forum for discussion of such issues. If you are the single person, entering into this situation could put you squarely in the middle of a married couple and allow you to be privy to secrets that belong to them alone. This is not a place where you should be. If you are the married person, you should really be restricting such discussions to your spouse or to someone you trust of the same sex. It is unfair of you to ask a single person to come between you and your spouse.

If both of you are married, this problem is doubled. Now, you have two people tinkering with two different marriages. This is a recipe for confusion and suspicion. Personal and intimate conversations should be discouraged and deflected back to either the spouse or someone of the same sex.

When to Say No

Just like professionals, you have the right to refuse to enter into an informal counseling situation if it is inappropriate or has a high possibility of becoming so. The need of the other person certainly is a factor, but you must weigh your other relationships and obligations to determine whether you can responsibly say yes to a request for serious counseling.

If you have a problem with lust, you should avoid any personal, informal counseling situation with a member of the opposite sex, especially one to whom you feel an immediate attraction. An alcoholic doesn't go into a tavern. A former smoker doesn't sit in the smoking section. Some things you simply cannot do. Accept your limitations. The obligations of friendship do not require self-destructive behavior.

Know Your Friend

An informal counseling situation is not the best way to make a friend. Instead, a friendship should already be well established. Then, it will be able to better withstand the effects of partnering, caring, and position.

Good friends have probably already worked out how to partner with each other without adding a sexualized component to their relationship. Good friends are used to caring for each other as a matter of course and within the proper context. Good friends are more likely to relate to each other from roughly equal positions. Good friends have also probably known each other over a long span of time and are aware of the other primary relationships in each other's lives.

By knowing well the person with whom you are considering entering into an informal counseling situation, you minimize the possibility of this person being a sexual manipulator or climber. If they were, these characteristics probably would have already manifested themselves.

Even knowing the person well, though, is no guarantee. Diligence on your part is still vital. Take the following steps if you are in an informal counseling situation.

1. Be alert to signs of sexualization, including the content of inner feelings, both in the other person and in yourself. Being in a deep relationship with the other person may cause latent feelings to surface.

192

2. Don't allow a crisis mode to shift your boundaries. Informal counseling situations are no less intense than many professional ones. If a crisis of some magnitude is fueling a need for the informal counseling relationship, be aware of the tendency to suspend normal relationship boundaries for the duration of the crisis. These boundaries need to be constantly reinforced to both parties.

3. If you feel uncomfortable with the content of the conversation, stop and disengage from the other person. If at anytime you feel the relationship is going in a direction you are not comfortable with, voice your feelings and disengage from the relationship. If this person really is your friend, they should understand and accept your decision.

———— Fuel for Thought ————

"Confess your sins to each other and pray for each other so that you may be healed," the Bible instructs us. "The prayer of a righteous man is powerful and effective" (James 5:16). God intends for us to go to each other when we need help, whether in a professional setting or an informal one. He expects us to do so without adding an inappropriately sexualized component. Whichever side of a counseling situation we find ourselves in, we are responsible for conducting that relationship appropriately. We are responsible to God to obey his rules concerning relationships and sex.

Take a moment and, in your notebook or binder, write down your responses to the following questions.

1. If you have ever gone to a professional counselor, therapist, doctor, or attorney for help with a personal problem, was the professional a member of the opposite sex? Why did you choose that particular person? Was sex a factor in your decision? How so?

2. Do you feel more comfortable opening up to a member of the same sex or opposite sex? Why do you think that is?

3. If you are a professional, what percentage of same- versus opposite-sex clients do you have? Are you more comfortable in a professional situation with one over the other? If so, why?

4. Have you ever been in a professional counseling situation that had to be terminated? Why?

5. Have you ever or are you currently in an informal counseling situation with a person of the opposite sex? How long have you been in this relationship?

6. Have you ever felt sexually attracted to this person during the course of your relationship? If so, what did you do?

7. Have you ever terminated an informal counseling situation with someone because of the introduction of a sexualized component? How did you feel about ending the relationship this way?

8. Look back at the story of Samson and Delilah on page 180. Samson ignored plenty of warning signs of Delilah's true intent for establishing and continuing their relationship. List at least three ways Samson was irresponsible in his conduct with Delilah.

MAY GOD ALWAYS DIRECT YOU *to just the right person to fill your need for advice and counsel. May you be wise whenever you enter into a new relationship or enter a new phase of a current relationship. May the Spirit of God always be the Counselor you turn to for help and inspiration.*

THOSE WHO WORK IN
SPIRITUAL REALMS CAN
ALSO GET CAUGHT UP
IN THE PHYSICAL.

13

A fool finds no pleasure in understanding but delights in airing his own opinions.
—Proverbs 18:2

RECOGNIZE
THE POWER OF THE PULPIT

Spiritual Heights Can Lead to Physical Falls

The tide was about to turn. He could feel it. For twenty-five years he'd been able to read the attitude of the people, had felt the pressure of their thoughts like a pulse. They'd believed him, up to now. But the wave had crested. He sensed the motionless arc of the swell. Yes, the tide was about to turn and head the opposite way. The tide was going out, and he was going with it.

Twenty-five years of bearing the vision for the church. Twenty-five years of straining to pull the weak, the lukewarm, closer to the goal, his goal, of what the church should be. Twenty-five years of hard work, late hours, too much time in meetings, too little time with his family. Twenty-five years of praying for them, sweating for them, sacrificing for them.

Twenty-five years and he could feel their mood turn against him, a rising groundswell of disbelief and betrayal. In his quiet moments of meditation he realized how much he could identify with Jesus as the crowd decided instead for a thief named Barabbas. Yes, he could now identify with the suffering of Jesus, but it gave him no joy. He desperately wanted to go back to identifying with Jesus as head of the church.

He was owed something for all of his time, energy, and direction. It was his drive and determination that had turned a small, fledgling congregation into a large, nationally recognized, spiritual force. Thousands of people had listened to his sermons, read his books, visited his church. Thousands of people had found Jesus through him. That ought to be worth something, shouldn't it? Whatever happened to loyalty?

He was constantly putting up his own life as an example of how one could overcome and conquer through the power of God. He'd never claimed to be perfect, often using his own shortcomings and foibles as sermon illustrations. It helped to balance his image as the spiritual head of the church with his imperfect, human nature.

After twenty-five years of dealing with the trials and tribulations of others, he certainly was well aware of imperfect, human nature. When he thought back about all the people whose lives he'd helped turn around, it made him angry to think they now had the self-righteous audacity to condemn him. Back when they'd brought their problems, their broken lives, to him to fix, he hadn't condemned them. He had done everything he could to help them. Very few people, he knew, could have provided such valuable counsel to all of those hurting people over the years.

He'd helped so many. Why was it necessary to dwell on just a few unfortunate incidents? One of which was completely false. Never happened. Whole thing was an out-and-out lie meant to destroy him. Some people in the church were envious of his position, just looking for any excuse to get him out of the way in their own rise to power. The other incidents, well, most of those had happened years ago, when he was younger and still struggling with how to put all of his roles as preacher, pastor, counselor, friend, and man into perspective. He acknowledged he hadn't always handled every situation perfectly. A few times, the people he'd counseled had gone away confused about the nature of his intentions. It was bound to happen, given the number of situations and the number of years.

The timing was just so bad for all of this to come out now. It had to be Satan's way of attacking his church. They were in the third year of a five-year expansion. Forward momentum was critical at this phase. Plans had been drawn, loans had been secured, construction had started, expectations had been tapped. And now, this.

For twenty-five years he'd been working toward this dream. Now, every morning he woke up in the middle of a nightmare. With all of his heart, he just wanted it to go away.

PULPITS AND PITFALLS

Across the country, denominations and congregations are dealing with the sexual misdeeds of trusted church leaders. Those who work in spiritual realms can also get caught up in the physical. The reasons for this paradox are as complicated, and as simple, as human nature.

The Pitfall of Spiritual Rule-Giving

When you are constantly in a position of articulating what is spiritually acceptable and unacceptable, the temptation exists to write a separate set of rules for yourself. The closeness of spiritual leaders to God and his work allows them to believe they have become favored children or the teacher's pet—in other words someone who is allowed to operate outside the normal rules. In this favored state, all they have to do is relay the rules, not obey them. It is a devious pitfall a pastor can slide into while feeling faithful and successful in ministry.

Through years of study spiritual leaders become increasingly familiar with the Bible, God's rulebook. One axiom warns us that familiarity breeds contempt. Could this be true for some who are most familiar with God's laws? Somewhere, over the course of time,

God's rules become their rules. God's authority becomes their authority. As leaders in the church, they focus more on their authority over others and less on their submission to God. They function like spiritual grounding wires. God's spiritual directives flow out through them, but they are somehow untouched by them.

They not only interpret what the Bible said at the time it was written but they also translate those rules into contemporary directives. In order to do this, they must use all of their knowledge and spiritual insights to assess the contemporary situation and respond with an appropriate biblical prohibition or principle. The danger comes when this interpretive skill is used not to direct others but to let themselves off the hook. They wind up using their ability to interpret and articulate God's word to develop two sets of criteria—one for themselves and one for everyone else.

At some point, of course, this dichotomy is uncovered. The duplicity of their words versus their actions becomes increasingly noticeable. Two of the most glaring examples of this type of behavior are the former televangelists Jim Bakker and Jimmy Swaggart. Both men reigned over vast spiritual empires, gaining thousands of converts and bringing in millions of dollars. Both were known to preach hard-line, convicting sermons. Both failed, spectacularly, to practice what they preached.

Jim Bakker's troubles were both sexual and financial. His arrogance led him both to break his marital vows through infidelity and to betray fiduciary arrangements made with thousands of well-meaning investors in a variety of financial schemes. When his finances came under scrutiny, an unusual payment of money was discovered. Bakker had used ministry funds to pay for the silence of a former female employee with whom he was having an affair. He was forced to admit to the affair, which finally cost him his marriage and his ministry. His financial dealings cost him his freedom, and he spent several years in prison for fraud.

It wasn't long after the newspapers were full of the Jim Bakker scandal that another Jim came under fire for his behavior. This time the Jim was Jimmy Swaggart, a driven, emotional, demonstrative, damnation-preaching televangelist. When evidence of his sexual indiscretions with a prostitute was unearthed, Swaggart went before his congregation and his television audience with a gut-wrenching admission of failure. While he did not give specifics, his tearful "I have sinned" admission seemed to stem the flood of followers leaving him.

Jimmy Swaggart's ministry was finally obliterated when it became known he was continuing his pattern of aberrant sexual sin. The first time Swaggart was confronted by his behavior, he told the world he'd sinned. The second time, he basically told the world it wasn't any of their business. While still proclaiming God's rules, Swaggart decided to violate those rules and exist in his own reality, a place where his behavior was somehow acceptable. By living as if he could operate under a second, different set of rules, he decimated his authority to articulate the first.

The Pitfall of Moral Balance

When constantly engaged in doing "the Lord's work," a pastor may be tempted to rationalize personal, sinful behavior by balancing out the bad with all of the good. People who use this scheme to rationalize misbehavior can hide from the real evil of their sins. As long as the good side of the scale is heavier than the bad side, they sense no spiritual jeopardy.

This pitfall has ensnared many spiritual leaders, not just pastors. Anyone who spends a lot of time in the work of the church is susceptible to thinking they are building up spiritual credits that can then be spent to redeem personal sin. They may acknowledge the behavior is sinful but argue that sin is inevitable. God knows this and takes it into account, they say. Instead of blaming them God is looking at their true motives, which they say are shown through the evidence of the majority of their actions. If, taken on balance, their good actions outweigh their inevitable bad ones, God's grace will cover the rest.

Under this rationale, even an inappropriately sexualized relationship can be spiritually atoned for through doing the "work of the church." Often the need to counterbalance the sin in their lives directly motivates these sinners to work even harder for the Lord. When these individuals are discovered, the overwhelming response of the congregation is one of disbelief. The glare of the visible examples of the leader's hard work for the church can blind their followers to the light of the truth. In turn, the loyalty of their fellow-believers adds weight to the good side of the scale, making it harder for such leaders to accept the truth about their sin.

The Pitfall of Comparison

It was finally time, no way to put it off any longer. He should have been preaching, instead he was resigning. It was either that or be fired. They'd at least given him the option of stepping down. Had the audacity to tell him it was for the good of the church! What else had he devoted his life to for the past twenty-five years, for heaven's sake?

He was going, and they were staying. He'd been there longer than any of them. It was his church more than it was theirs. He'd invested more time, more energy, more dreams than the lot of them. They'd said he could stay after he resigned. All he had to do was publicly repent and confess his sins before the congregation. They wanted to help him, they said.

They wanted to help him? He shook his head in disbelief. For twenty-five years, it had been him helping them! Now, looking out over the audience, he looked into the faces of those he'd pastored. He knew all of their stories, all of their sins. There they were, gazing up at him, waiting for him to tell them, waiting for him to explain.

Well, he wasn't going to. He wasn't going to dignify the allegations with a direct response. He outlined, in general terms, the difficulty to the congregation, the upheaval to the plans for new construction, the need to move on and put all of the unpleasantness behind them, his need to spend time with family right now—all as reasons for his departure. He reiterated his innocence of the charges while allowing for the possibility that it was all a vast case of confusion and misunderstanding being used by the sinfully motivated.

He kept his composure through all of it, remaining calm on the outside. Inside, however, he was seething. It was an affront to everything he'd ever worked for to have to be up there at all, especially in front of all these people who had done far greater harm, and far less good, than he.

When constantly confronted with the evil deeds of others, the temptation exists to rationalize sinful behavior by the delusion that God grades on a curve. The temptation exists to think God looks out at all of humanity and compares each person to every other person. With this pitfall, as long as your behavior is "above average," you are in no spiritual jeopardy.

Those who spend a good deal of their time counseling or working with those coming to grips with their own spiritual filthiness may begin to view themselves as being spiritually clean by comparison. Further, since their overall appearance is so clean, one or two minor spots may not seem to significantly foul their spiritual garb.

The Pitfall of Playing God

Because they are constantly confronted by individuals seeking spiritual guidance and absolution for sin in their lives, some pastors may be tempted to seek personal benefits from their position of trust.

People who are seeking God's grace reach a terrible moment when they comprehend their lost condition. The realization of being outside of God's protection can produce an intense reaction of fear and hopelessness. They are not unlike the crowd in the second chapter of the Book of Acts who recognized they had crucified the Son of God. "When the people heard this, they were cut to the heart and said to Peter and the other apostles, 'Brothers, what shall we do?'" (Acts 2:37). Spiritual leaders today hear the same cry as Peter. In moments of moral weakness, they can be tempted to ask the naive seekers to serve them in immoral ways in order to receive spiritual redemption.

Fear produces desperation. Desperation crumples boundaries because desperate people do desperate things. When people are desperate to save themselves, normal rules no longer seem to apply. The pull of self-preservation overrides other concerns. The person who is falling to his death will let go of important things in order to clutch a rope. Many spiritual leaders extend the rope of forgiveness to their followers. The unscrupulous leader may ask for things of great value in exchange for that rope.

Nowhere is this pitfall more evident than in the case of the abuse of young boys by some Catholic priests. Within the Catholic faith, priests not only interpret the Bible for their followers; they also hear private confession and assign actions to absolve the confessor of guilt. This gives a priest a degree of authority over his followers unknown in most mainstream Protestant churches. Catholic followers who believe in the need for absolution show an extreme amount of trust in and obedience to the words of their priest.

Within this climate of authority and trust, horrendous crimes have been committed. Over the past several years the Catholic church has had to admit moral failure by their priests on an alarming scale. Hundreds of men across the country have come forward to accuse priests of sexually abusing them years before when they served the church as altar boys. The priests would befriend them, often replacing an absent or distant father. Within this cultivated relationship of trust and spiritual guidance, the priest would introduce a sexual component. Some of the boys say they were molested. Others were groomed for a more extended sexual relationship with the priest.

Because the priest holds the keys to spiritual absolution and personal humiliation, most of the abused kept the truth of what happened to them a secret for years. When they grew up, some stayed faithful to the church, but others shunned religion altogether. As often happens, one man finally told what had been done to him. Then, another. And another. Before long, stories began to appear across the country in newspapers and magazines. The Catholic church, so long denying the widespread nature of the abuse, finally acknowledged the scandal and set up a national hotline to field calls from abuse victims.

While our minds reel at the extent of this abuse, we are also incredulous at first that so many would stay silent for so long. Personal shame certainly was one reason. But many victims still continued to insist their priest cared about them, even loved them, regardless of the abuse they were describing. Their memories of the events included both moments of extreme agony and times of companionship and caring. For many of the victims the climate of trust and authority built up by the priest dissipated slowly, fed by their own need for denial. It will take years for many of these now-adult men to come to grips with their past abuse.

The sin and resulting damage are just as great, of course, if the clerical abuser is a Methodist youth minister or a Lutheran choir director. Protestant sins hurt just as bad as Catholic ones. The Catholic ones just made more recent national headlines. From the time when the wicked sons of Eli the priest slept with the female attendants of the holy tent of meeting, some representatives of God have offended him and disgraced their calling through sexual sin in holy places. Stories like *Elmer Gantry* and *Marjoe* reflect an unsavory side of ministry none of us should ever be a part of.

THE PROBLEM WITH A TWO-FACED LIFE

Church leaders often take great care to present a certain image or to project a particular persona from the pulpit or from another position of authority. The public face is presented without blemish as an example to others of how to live a righteous life. The public face is confident, in control, calm in the face of danger, beyond the ravages of sin. The public face is open and may even talk in general terms about personal sin, but only in the after sense of a before-and-after picture setting. As if to say, yes, I had this sin but I've gotten past it, and you can too. The public face is cultivated to show the best possible side, minus the warts and blemishes of reality.

No one can live their entire life with just a public face. The private face eventually comes out, in quiet moments, at home with family, or in times of stress or fatigue. The more pressure we feel to present the public face, the worse our private face may become. The stress of trying to be someone you are not can be extremely draining. As we all know, it is not our best nature that comes out when we are stressed or tired. Just ask a parent who's been up three nights in a row with a colicky baby if they've been getting enough sleep lately. You're bound to get a thoroughly honest answer.

The other problem with being two-faced—with having a distinct and separate public and private persona—is how we attempt to allow the public persona to reign supreme. Since the public persona is the "righteous" one, it is naturally the one we want to present at all times. The problem this causes for church leaders in particular is one of isolation. If the private face is the one that mirrors fatigue, impatience, and imperfection, then the private face must only be shown to a select few, usually family. Because it is impossible to constantly keep the private face hidden behind the public face, a church leader may begin to limit contact with people outside of the select inner few. Some church leaders find themselves interacting with thousands of people but having few close friends. Instead of solving the problem, isolation only intensifies the division between the public and private faces. Jesus had something to say about two-faced religious leaders. He called them "hypocrites."

Four Eyes Can Still Be Blind

Being two-faced can wind up propelling you straight into a pitfall we described earlier—the pitfall of spiritual rule-giving. The public face is used to articulate what is or is not spiritually acceptable. This two-faced role allows for the fragmentation of spiritual rules into public and private categories, into a set of rules for everyone else (the public) and a separate set of rules for yourself (the private). The public face articulates the rules, and the private face alters them for personal benefit.

In what we have called the pitfall of moral balance, the public and private personas are weighed. If the good of the public face outweighs the bad of the private face, then acceptable moral balance appears to be achieved and personal sin can be rationalized. If you have spent the last four days speaking at a revival meeting, for example, then you can be in moral balance if you missed your daughter's graduation or your son's award, or if you yell at your wife because you're tired when you get off the plane.

In our roles as church leaders, we have maximum opportunity to project our public faces while viewing the private faces of others. Others come to us in times of great stress and trial in their lives when they are barely able to function, let alone to worry about their public and private faces. Pretense is often shattered in the trauma of the moment. Given this dichotomy, it is easy for us to fall into the pitfall of comparison. Their unvarnished private faces of grief, despair, anguish, and sin can make our pristine public faces look even better by comparison. They even make our less-than-pretty private faces seem not so bad.

This may tempt us into the fourth pitfall of playing God. When even your private face begins to look good compared to the private lives of others, the danger of self-righteousness looms large. We may even begin to see all of our lives as really being lived out in that prideful, perfect, public face. When we perceive ourselves as so good, even our detestable behavior can be rationalized. Somehow, we've risen above the muck of the physical, the private, and exist in the rarified air of the spiritual, the public. In this pitfall, we actually go from playing God to feeling godlike. The other term for this is self-righteousness.

The Power of the Pulpit

In today's culture the possibility of anybody exercising absolute physical authority over another person has almost been eliminated. Relationships of all kinds operate under the scrutiny of community, state, and federal entities. Parents can no longer withhold basic needs from their children. Husbands can no longer legally beat their wives. Employers are now forbidden to exploit their workers. These actions would violate the rights of others.

We are a society of rights. Certain rights not only are protected; they have become ingrained in our collective consciousness. Authority in our culture is kept on a short leash. Children know they can tell a teacher if their parent hits them. Wives know they can have their husbands arrested for spousal abuse. Employees know they can file a complaint with their company or government agency if they are being exploited at work.

In one area, however, authority is still largely intact. The power of religion remains strong. For those who believe in God, the power of the pulpit is still a potent force, for good or evil. For those who profess faith, secular authority may be compromised, but spiritual authority still has clout.

WHO IS A SPIRITUAL LEADER?

For the most part, this chapter has focused on pastors or preachers. However, the pitfalls we've outlined can trip up any person who finds themselves in a position of spiritual guidance or authority over another. Certainly, this would include church elders, ministry leaders, and church workers in general.

Anytime a person submits to your authority in a church or in a spiritually related matter or task, you become a spiritual leader to that person. For one time, or for a lifetime, these temptations and pitfalls are present and possible if you stand in that role. Do not be deceived into thinking it is only prominent, highly visible church leaders who need to beware of these pitfalls. At the same time, do not be deceived into thinking that only those who are unaccustomed to wielding spiritual authority can fall into temptation in these areas.

——— Fuel for Thought ———

All spiritual leaders need to be aware constantly of the power they hold over those in their spiritual care, whether the leadership role is temporary or long-lasting. Spiritual leaders also must never lose sight of the power sin can hold over them in times of spiritual weakness. A confluence of these factors can lead to spiritual betrayal and abuse.

As you consider your role as a spiritual leader, keep the following questions in mind:

1. Are you currently involved in a church? If not, why not?
2. Whether or not you attend a church, do you see yourself as a spiritual leader?
3. Do other people come to you often asking for spiritual advice or counsel? Do you offer that advice?
4. Have you ever asked for anything in return for that advice? If so, what did you ask for?

5. If you are a spiritual leader in a congregation, what is your function?

6. As a spiritual leader, what are your sexual boundaries? How do you deal with your inappropriate thoughts?

7. How do people inside your congregation relate to you as a spiritual leader?

8. How do people outside your congregation relate to you as a spiritual leader?

9. After reviewing the pitfalls mentioned in this chapter, which do you feel you need to be especially aware of?

10. Have you ever found yourself in a situation where you have been tempted to operate by a different set of rules than those around you? How did you feel?

11. Make a list of the advice you have given to others but have not followed yourself.

12. Has anyone ever confronted you with sin in your own life? How did you respond to that person?

13. If you gave reasons or made excuses for your behavior, what were they? Did any of them correspond to one of the pitfalls listed in this chapter?

When we are in the midst of certain situations, the rules somehow can become cloudy. Rules are much clearer when they apply to someone else. It is natural to be rigid with others and flexible with ourselves. Our capacity for rationalizing and excusing our own behavior is vast. When this capacity is combined with the power of sexual gratification, a dangerous situation is present.

MAY GOD'S WORD STEER YOU *to consistency in what you say and what you do. May you never rely on your own wisdom but only on the Lord's. May you be blind to self and focused on God. May he grant you clarity of vision to see yourself and others as he does.*

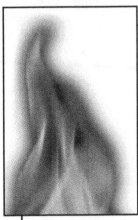

ELI'S SONS WERE WICKED MEN; they had no regard for the LORD.

This sin of the young men was very great in the LORD's sight, for they were treating the LORD's offering with contempt.

But Samuel was ministering before the LORD—a boy wearing a linen ephod. Each year his mother made him a little robe and took it to him when she went up with her husband to offer the annual sacrifice. Eli would bless Elkanah and his wife, saying, "May the LORD give you children by this woman to take the place of the one she prayed for and gave to the LORD." Then they would go home. And the LORD was gracious to Hannah; she conceived and gave birth to three sons and two daughters. Meanwhile, the boy Samuel grew up in the presence of the LORD.

Now Eli, who was very old, heard about everything his sons were doing to all Israel and how they slept with the women who served at the entrance to the Tent of Meeting. So he said to them, "Why do you do such things? I hear from all the people about these wicked deeds of yours. No, my sons; it is not a good report that I hear spreading among the LORD's people. If a man sins against another man, God may mediate for him; but if a man sins against the LORD, who will intercede for him?" His sons, however, did not listen to their father's rebuke, for it was the LORD's will to put them to death.

—from 1 Samuel 2

14

A discerning man
keeps wisdom in view,
but a fool's eyes wander
to the ends of the earth.
—Proverbs 17:24

AVOID

A CHURCH BURNING

Use Spiritual Flame Retardant

She was new to even the idea of faith and so
eager to learn, to please. Jack couldn't get
over how well she always did her Bible study, week after week. If
only some of the members at church would take their study as seriously! She was never even a minute late to their meetings. Her
bright face would peek into his office, Bible clutched tightly in her
hands, like clockwork, every Wednesday afternoon. It got to where
it wouldn't be a Wednesday without her.

She asked a lot of questions about the Bible and God, naturally,
but she also seemed curious about the church and how things
worked. His duties were of particular interest to her. At least once
each week, she would thank him for taking a personal interest in
her, especially with all of his other responsibilities. Consistently, he
reiterated her importance to God and explained it was his privilege
to teach her the truth of Scripture.

Yes, she seemed so willing to learn. Everything was going along
fine, at least as far as he could tell. He'd been working with her
about four and a half months when the bottom dropped out. On a

Saturday night two of the elders came to talk to him about her. He'd been completely blindsided. According to them, she'd gone to the elders of the church and accused him of pressuring her to have sex during their sessions together.

For a moment, he couldn't even respond; his mouth just hung open in shock. She did what? It didn't make any sense. Why would Jeannine say such a thing? The elders had come to him to find out the answer to that very question. Starting from the first time he'd met her, he went back over, for them and for himself, each of his actions, all of the times they'd been together. It was bewildering to have to remember almost five months of meetings, discussions, items of study. Because he was so shocked, it took him several minutes to reconstruct the hours upon hours of interaction with Jeannine.

At some point, Patty appeared out of the back of the house, a look of consternation furrowing her brows. They'd been speaking in hushed tones, but she sensed something was wrong. Maybe it was the look on their faces when Mike and Stan had come in. She was much more attuned to that sort of thing than he was. This was one of the reasons they made such a great pair in ministry. Sitting down on the arm of his chair, she joined in, not by saying anything but by being present at his side. Jack was impressed with how she handled the whole thing. Never once did she think the charge could be anything but a terrible mistake. Her only concern was to get to the bottom of it, to uncover the truth she knew was there.

The charge was false. That was the truth.

Jack didn't know how he would have handled it if Patty hadn't been there for him that night, so steadfast in her belief in his innocence. He didn't know what he would have done if it had been some distant church officials—strangers—who showed up at his door instead of Stan and Mike. They were church elders, sure, but they were also good friends and partners in prayer. The next several weeks wouldn't be easy, but together they'd get safely to the other side of it all.

IT COULD HAPPEN TO YOU

Some of you reading this right now are nodding your heads. This very thing has happened to you. As a church leader you've been accused of inappropriate sexual behavior with someone, probably in your church. You've found yourself having to go back over your actions and explain them to others. You've had to look into the faces of people who believed you, who didn't believe you, into the faces of those who just weren't sure.

Some of you reading this right now are shaking your heads. Nothing like this has ever happened to you. You can't imagine what it would be like to be accused of wrongdoing in this way. Maybe, as you think back over the past, you realize you've been close to a problem a time or two, but this isn't a situation you've ever had to face personally.

Whether you've experienced something like this firsthand, if you're still in ministry, it could happen to you again. By taking precautions now, you can reduce the risk of being accused of improper behavior. You can set the groundwork for the truth of your innocence to be known if an accusation should ever be made. You need to take a proactive position and integrate certain behaviors into your life and ministry to help fortify your boundaries.

Be Pure

Before the truth of your innocence can be known, of course, you have to be innocent. Simply put, you need to flee from sexual immorality of any kind. All the time. You know how powerful sexual attraction and lust can be. If you have forgotten, reread Proverbs, especially chapters 7 through 9. Your ability to lead God's people will be fatally compromised if your reputation mirrors that of Eli's sons. Commit to sexual purity by fortifying yourself in God's word. Remind yourself of the dangers of sexual immorality. Remind yourself, also, of the rewards of marital love. Reread the Song of Solomon and recommit to preserving your sexuality for the area God approves.

Because of the power of sin, and especially sexual sin, it is not enough to say it won't happen to you or that you'll be able to resist if tempted. You must continually renew your commitment to sexual purity through prayer. Before you enter into a situation where temptation might be present, give yourself, the others you'll be with, and the situation to God. If you have been sexually tempted as a church leader, give that to God in prayer. With the repentant, honest heart of David, cry out to God for strength and guidance.

Be Accountable

The reason evil likes the darkness instead of the light is because darkness hides evil deeds and light exposes them. One of the most effective ways for any church leader to bring light into their ministry is to have an accountability group. If you have a tendency to hide, an accountability group can make sure that light penetrates even the darkest places.

Such a group could be drawn from a variety of places. You can meet with a group of people from your own church (generally of the same gender) who agree to meet and pray with you. You become accountable to them for your Christian walk in general, and for how you are conducting yourself as a church leader in particular. They benefit you by lovingly shining light onto your life and ministry. Carefully choose mature Christians who are not intimidated by your position as a church leader.

You might also meet with a group of church leaders from your denomination or branch of faith. You would agree to be accountable to each other for how you conduct your Christian lives and your ministries. A group like this would bring the value of experience in

holding you accountable for your actions. As church leaders themselves, they would be familiar with the temptations and struggles
inherent in church ministry.

Some pastors find it easier to be completely open with a group
of their colleagues who have no formal tie to their congregation or
denomination. Total honesty in an accountability group implies
total trust of all the members of the group. Who can blame a pastor
who finds it hard to be truly transparent in the presence of people
who may vote to continue or terminate his ministry a few weeks
later.

Since there never seems to be an abundance of prayer, you may
choose to meet with several groups for prayer, guidance, and
accountability in your ministry. Before you do so, however, it will
be necessary to remove any vestige of hiding behind a public facade.
Accountability groups cannot function optimally if you are trying
to whitewash the truth and to present only a public face. For your
groups to pray for and with you most effectively, you will need to
work on becoming more and more transparent.

Be Transparent

The public face tries to hide the brokenness of the private face
as if something was shameful about being broken before God and
men. The world says that to be a leader, you must be strong, intact.
Brokenness is unacceptable to the world. Brokenness, however, is
acceptable and pleasing to God. "The sacrifices of God are a broken
spirit," the psalmist prayed. "A broken and contrite heart, O God,
you will not despise" (Psalm 51:17). Being transparent to God,
regardless of what face we wear, is the only sensible approach, for he
is completely aware of our brokenness. Attempting to be two-faced
before a God who sees all is both foolish and useless. Transparency
is the only option.

Instead of trying to live with two faces, all of us must strive to
live transparently with each other and with our own selves.

Transparency allows us to realize we have a spiritual side and a sinful nature that coexist. By keeping the two side by side, not artificially separated, we are constantly reminded of the choices we must make either to follow God or to follow our own sinful desires. Such is the spiritual battle each of us engages in daily. This is why we need all the reinforcements we can get through accountability groups.

Transparency to others allows them to see when we are struggling or hurting and come to our aid. Remember, James 5:16 tells us to confess our sins to each other. There is a very good reason for doing this: We are not only forced to own up to our behavior, but those who have heard our confession can then pray for us so that we may be healed. When we refuse to confess our sins, we cut ourselves off from the double blessings of prayer and healing.

Trying to hide sin with the charade of public faces obscures the transparency of God living within us. When others look at us, they are to see God, not because we are so good or righteous but because our lives should be clear enough for God in us to show through. The mystery is that people can see us and God in us at the same time. The marvel of this mystery builds up our faith and attracts those who are searching for truth.

Be Aware

The pitfalls outlined in the previous chapter pose grave dangers to church leaders when sexual temptation is being used to dig the pit. If as a church leader for example, you are already used to operating under two sets of rules (that's the pitfall of spiritual rule-giving, remember, with the first set of rules preached to others and the second for yourself), the temptation will be great to extend these dual behavioral codes to sexual situations. As a result, you may preach a doctrine of sexual purity to others while engaging in your own sexual sins.

In the cascading descent of sexual sins, in order to justify this tension between the two sets of rules, you may rationalize your sexual indiscretions, using mental games to balance them against all of the good work you are doing for the church. You may say to yourself that sleeping with Ed's wife isn't so bad because, after all, you helped Ed overcome his alcoholism. Since Ed doesn't know about you and his wife but is very much aware of the benefits of his sobriety, in the balance Ed's life is better. You may say to yourself that the thrill you receive from discussing intimate, detailed, sexual information while counseling young women about to be married isn't wrong because in the balance you are helping them prepare for their future as sexually active wives. You may say to yourself that fondling a teen isn't really that bad because of the great need adolescents have for tenderness and affection.

As you work toward attaining moral balance for your deeds, you may attempt to make the bad seem less bad. By comparing your acts of sexualization to other sins, you may seek to lighten their weight on the scale. In this rationale, if you are engaged in inappropriately sexual conversation, that isn't as bad as physical touching. If you are engaged in inappropriately sexual physical contact, that isn't as bad as actual intercourse. If you are engaged in actual intercourse, that isn't as bad as acts of physical violence that would cause visible signs of abuse.

If all else fails to allow you to rationalize your sexualized behavior, you may decide you are somehow due compensation for all of the good you are doing. If your late nights of church work are keeping you away from home, away from your bed at night, you may decide you are justified in sleeping with someone you are working with at the church. In this rationale, if the church is keeping you from fulfilling your sexual desires, shouldn't the church be the one to compensate you for your loss? In the case of the Catholic priests we mentioned earlier, their vow of celibacy may have, in their minds, justified their sexual behavior. After all, they were abstaining from sex with women by expending their sexual desires with the young boys the church itself unintentionally made available.

As you stumble into each successive pitfall, you dig yourself a deeper and deeper hole and your rationalizations are less and less in touch with reality. Although God is able to redeem you from whatever pit you have got yourself into, the amount of time and energy it will take for you to crawl out from under the consequences of your behavior can be significant.

Sexual sins rarely remain stagnant. Their intoxicating nature demands continual, repeated, and increased doses. The more one engages in a sexual sin, the less potent that particular activity becomes. Sexual sins have a tendency to up the ante by fueling greater and greater deviant behavior, dragging us down into a gaping morass of compromise and depravity. Be extremely wary, then, about even advancing toward the edge of the abyss. You may find yourself sliding to the bottom into a pile of filth before you know it. Don't be like ancient Eli's sons, who refused counsel when their sins were rebuked. Do you remember what God did to punish them because they profaned their ministry?

Be Alert

You may be doing everything you can to avoid the dangers of sexualized relationships in your ministry. Whenever you deal with other people, however, you are not the only one involved. Your behavior may be flawless and your intentions impeccable, but the other person may have another agenda you know nothing about. So never let down your guard. Remain alert to sexual dangers at all times.

Christian psychiatrist Louis McBurney counsels ministers at Marble Retreat in Marble, Colorado. In an article titled "Seduced" in *Leadership Journal* (Fall 1998), he documents the sexual dangers a pastor may face. "In one situation I know," McBurney writes, "three successive pastors were terminated by the same church for immoral behavior with the same church musician. In each case, she lured the minister into an intimate relationship and then claimed he had raped her. I was convinced working with two of the three pastors that, as a pastor's daughter, she was acting out rage toward her father, who never had time for her."

Professional counselors employ common-sense precautions to reduce their risk of being accused of inappropriate sexual behavior with their clients. Some of these measures can be useful to spiritual counselors as well. Review the advice we gave earlier to professionals in chapter 12 and apply it to your situation in ministry or church-based relationships.

CHECKING THE DOOR FOR HEAT

Jesus wants his ministers to be smart and clean. "Be as shrewd as snakes and as innocent as doves," he bids us (Matthew 10:16). Even the purest-hearted pastoral counselors have to stay on their toes to avoid being compromised sexually. The desire that could land you in a problem doesn't have to be yours. It could belong to the person you are trying to help. Spiritual counselors tend to attract the confused, the tormented, and sometimes, the evil. In any potentially volatile counseling relationship, it is a good idea to constantly be checking the door for heat. The innocent look to their side and blithely say there is no fire. Open the door, however, and you could be engulfed in an inferno from the other side. Those who are spiritually shrewd concede the possibility of fire and check the door often for heat.

Dealing with the Confused

Stan and Mike left the house after several hours, leaving Jack and Patty totally exhausted. In the quiet of their den, they held each other while Jack whispered words of regret and dismay and Patty whispered back words of encouragement and belief. They were going to get through this. Without doing so consciously, both of them began to pray. Together they prayed for themselves, for the church, for Stan and Mike, for the rest of the elders, for the truth to be known, and for Jeannine.

Jack didn't understand all of what was going on, but he was deeply concerned about Jeannine. Something had to be wrong for her to make such a charge. He didn't think she was evil, just that she was a very confused young woman. With God's help, Stan and Mike would find out the reason for her accusation. With God's help, Jack would be vindicated and Jeannine would be helped. He fervently prayed that this would be so.

Jack had to admit that it was an uncomfortable position to be in, especially for someone who was used to being in control of things at the church. He would have to step aside and allow God to lead Stan, Mike, and the other elders to the truth. His role now was one of prayer and support. It was bad enough going through this knowing he was innocent. He couldn't imagine the guilt, shame, and devastation he would be suffering if what Jeannine was accusing had actually happened.

Nothing like this had ever happened to him before. But he had to admit that it shook him to the core.

Some of the people who may come to you for spiritual guidance will be confused. Confused about their spirituality. Confused about their sexuality. Confused about life in general. In their confusion, the ability to maintain their own personal boundaries, if they even have any, could become severely compromised. They may intermix God's love for them with sexual love. As God's representative in their eyes, you may become a target of their confused sexual response to God's spiritual love.

For people who are this confused, a same-sex spiritual counselor is probably the best answer. Some people, because of their upbringing or habitual patterns, can only relate to a meaningful, in-depth relationship with someone of the opposite sex in sexual terms. If the only way they have previously dealt with opposite-sex authority figures was through sexualization, this pattern may overlay any relationship they have with you. They may introduce a sexual component to your relationship as a comfort mechanism for themselves. If they can sexualize the relationship, it becomes something they are used to dealing with. The more out of control or confused they feel during the course of your counseling relationship, the stronger may be their desire to return the relationship to a forum they are familiar with.

Dealing with the Tormented

At this point, their confusion could take them one step farther. It may not be enough for them to attempt to introduce a sexual component into your relationship. Even if you do not actually respond, they still may fantasize a relationship with you. They harbor a deep need for this fantasy to be the truth. This fantasy could include attributing double meanings to words you use, sexualized meanings to actions you take, double entendres to advice you give. Their determination to have your sexual attention could fuel them to manufacture attraction out of innocence on your part.

It is not always possible to recognize such a tormented soul when they first enter your world. They are usually adept at controlling their desires and manipulating perceptions. At first, they will be quite happy merely to be in your presence. Your just taking time to speak with them or to meet with them will be seen as proof of your true attraction. As a consequence, they will appear positive, responsive, and eager to please.

Over time, however, the nature of their intentions should begin to leak out. They may attempt to redirect the basis of your conversations from them to you. Their responses to you may seem out of place, overly enthusiastic. Their facial expressions, vocalizations, and body language may change during the course of your relationship as their sexual fantasies regarding you increasingly overlay the reality of that relationship.

During this time, of course, the possibility always exists they will come to realize how wrong they have been and begin to work on modifying their behavior toward you. Clarity is always possible in the midst of confusion, especially when you effectively cause God's light to penetrate personal darkness.

Some, however, will lash out when it becomes obvious to them that you really don't have any sexual regard for them. Remember, in their mind, you are already fantasy lovers. When reality sinks in, they may strike out against you as a lover scorned. And the poet was right: Hell has no greater fury. Where they were compliant and eager to please before, now they may become vindictive and eager to harm. Rarely are they reluctant, at this stage, to drag others into the situation if by doing so they can add to your personal harm. Obviously, these confused and tormented individuals can cause a great deal of damage to individual church leaders and to the congregations they serve.

Dealing with the Evil

It is difficult to tell, at this point, whether the person you are dealing with is delusional or demonic or both. Whichever, they still need Jesus.

If they are evil, their purpose is to cause you to sin. When their initial attempts to subvert your morals are unsuccessful, they will use more blatant ways to compromise your spiritual boundaries. Evil can be difficult to spot initially, as long as it is mirroring good in order to hide. Eventually its true nature becomes increasingly visible.

Evil people should be confronted with their sin and their ungodly attempts to seduce others. They should be held accountable in the church for this behavior and called to repentance. If they can be made to see their sin and turn, you will have witnessed the saving grace of God fully at work. If, however, they refuse to admit to their sin and insist on continuing in it, you have no choice but to disfellowship them from the church. You can, by all means, continue to pray for their souls, but you must withdraw yourself from any relationship with them. If this action seems harsh to you, read 1 Corinthians 5. It outlines, in detail, the danger of allowing such a person to continue within your fellowship and the necessity for withdrawing from them.

If the person is not evil, but ill, that will become known in time as well. Their grasp of reality will be slippery on other details, not just about your relationship. The more you can get them to talk, the more the fantasy details will come out as they lose track of what actually occurred versus what they wanted to have happen. These discrepancies should give you a clue about their delusional state.

These are also glaring warning signs. Since most church leaders are not trained therapists, people like this need to be referred to competent professionals, sooner rather than later. This goes back to the "Just say no" suggestion. Certain people you simply are not equipped to deal with. If you are in doubt about whether a person is delusional or truly evil, strongly urge them to seek help from a Christian therapist who will be professionally trained to make a proper diagnosis and to offer appropriate aid. When you are making this referral, by all means look for a Christian professional of the same gender as the person you are trying to help.

——— Fuel for Thought ———

Living for Jesus means living in a constant state of spiritual warfare. Not only does an internal struggle rage between the spirit and the flesh, but an external struggle also goes on between the forces of good and the powers of darkness. As a spiritual leader you are on the front lines of both battles.

It is no coincidence, perhaps, that Paul includes the following instructions in his letter to the Ephesians right after a long section dealing with the relationships we find ourselves in. In Ephesians 6:10–18, he exhorts:

Finally, be strong in the Lord and in his mighty power. Put on the full armor of God so that you can take your stand against the devil's schemes. For our struggle is not against flesh and blood, but against the rulers, against the authorities, against the powers of this dark world and against the spiritual forces of evil in the heavenly realms. Therefore put on the full armor of God, so that when the day of evil comes, you may be able to stand your ground, and after you have done everything, to stand. Stand firm then, with the belt of truth buckled around your waist, with the breastplate of righteousness in place, and with your feet fitted with the readiness that comes from the gospel of peace. In addition to all this, take up the shield of faith, with which you can extinguish all the flaming arrows of the evil one. Take the helmet of salvation and the sword of the Spirit, which is the word of God. And pray in the Spirit on all occasions with all kinds of prayers and requests. With this in mind, be alert and always keep on praying for all the saints.

As a spiritual leader in the Lord's church, you need to be ready for battle whenever it presents itself, in whatever form it presents itself. Allow yourself to be caught unprotected, and disaster is sure to follow.

But glory be to God who has so marvelously shielded you in this battle with his armor. In your role as church leader, how would you use each of these items of spiritual armor to keep yourself from sexual sin:

1. The belt of truth?

2. The breastplate of righteousness?

3. The readiness from the gospel of peace?

4. The shield of faith?

5. The helmet of salvation?

6. The sword of the Spirit?

7. Prayer in the Spirit?

As a church leader you are on the front lines, representing God and Christ to the world. Your behavior, therefore, will be judged not only by the people who observe you but also by the God whose name you wear. Be careful how you wear it.

Helpful Resource: You are welcome to use our comprehensive Web site (www.aplaceofhope.com) to obtain services and products offered by The Center for Counseling and Health Resources, Inc., and to access Dr. Jantz.

MAY GOD'S SPIRIT GIVE YOU A DISCERNING EYE *with which to see the truth about people and situations. May his Spirit give you a resistant heart that turns to him instead of following evil. May he show you the rewards of your work to carry you through the dark hour of disappointment and failure. May the armor of God protect you each day as a leader in his church.*

JESUS WENT TO THE MOUNT OF OLIVES. At dawn he appeared again in the temple courts, where all the people gathered around him, and he sat down to teach them. The teachers of the law and the Pharisees brought in a woman caught in adultery. They made her stand before the group and said to Jesus, "Teacher, this woman was caught in the act of adultery. In the Law Moses commanded us to stone such women. Now what do you say?" They were using this question as a trap, in order to have a basis for accusing him.

But Jesus bent down and started to write on the ground with his finger. When they kept on questioning him, he straightened up and said to them, "If any one of you is without sin, let him be the first to throw a stone at her." Again he stooped down and wrote on the ground.

At this, those who heard began to go away one at a time, the older ones first, until only Jesus was left, with the woman still standing there. Jesus straightened up and asked her, "Woman, where are they? Has no one condemned you?"

"No one, sir," she said.

"Then neither do I condemn you," Jesus declared. "Go now and leave your life of sin."

—from John 8

15

Fear God and keep his
commandments.... For
God will bring every
deed into judgment,
including every hidden
thing, whether it
. is good or evil.
—Ecclesiastes 12:13–14

EMBRACING LIFE AND
RELATIONSHIPS WISELY

The scripture quoted above is for us as much as for those who first heard it centuries ago. These simple words distill our duty on earth: to fear God and keep his commandments. It took the ancient writer twelve chapters to come to this simple conclusion in his book. It has taken fourteen chapters to come to this simple conclusion of this book. If a relationship is not marriage, it should not be sexualized. The truth is that simple. God permits us to be sexual in one setting only—in marriage. God's word clarifies this simple command. Man's sin complicates it.

We started off by looking at the influence of culture on our sexual values and boundaries. We discussed the dynamics that allow partnering, unequal position, companionship, and compassion to cause relationships to become improperly sexual. We then looked at the risks involved when these factors are joined in secular and spiritual counseling situations. We also have seen how these factors can be perverted in family relationships. And we have discussed the boundaries necessary in opposite-sex relationships and the need for healthy same-sex relationships. *"Recognize* the danger of inappropriately sexualized relationships," we have warned in chapter after chapter. *"Avoid* and prepare for these dangers," we have counseled in chapter after chapter.

After all of these chapters, let's take just a moment to review.

HIGH-RISK SITUATIONS

Any time members of the opposite sex enter into a relationship together, whether at work, at play, at home, or at church, sexualization must be recognized as a risk.

Some situations carry a higher degree of risk than others. Intense work relationships carry a risk of forging an inappropriate partnering. Unequal position relationships carry a risk for one party to demand more than is acceptable and the other party to offer more than is appropriate. Unhealthy family relationships foster the risk of sexual aggression of the stronger on the weaker, the older on the younger. Companion relationships, with their warmth and comfortable nature, carry a risk for intimacy to be transferred inappropriately. Counseling relationships risk turning a motivation of compassion into an opportunity for passion. Unwise religious relationships may cause one or both parties to stumble morally.

By recognizing the risk inherent in these situations, you can more wisely determine whether to enter into them, and you can more effectively guard yourself from harm if you do.

Life is never without risk. God himself took a tremendous risk when he gave us free will. He runs the risk of losing each soul for eternity. If life—my life, your life—is worth the risk to God, then life and relationships need to be worth the risk to us. Just because the potential exists for relationships to become inappropriately sexualized, we need not hide away from the world and other people!

PROPER BOUNDARIES

But remember, it is not just the situation that must be assessed for danger. You must also examine yourself to be sure that your own ineffective or nonexistent personal boundaries do not compound your risk.

Before entering into any relationship, remember to have your personal boundaries firmly established. These boundaries are there to perform a twofold purpose: (1) They remind you of where you will not go and what you will not do, thereby restraining your personal behavior; and (2) these boundaries protect you against harmful action from the outside, shielding you from dangerous behaviors of others. They help you to know when it is necessary for you to speak up for yourself and speak out against unwanted actions. Our boundaries are made up of our personal convictions, system of values, and moral guidelines. Each boundary should be shaped and fortified by God's Word and will. Our personal behavior and ethical decisions are carried out within the security of these boundaries.

HIGH-RISK INDIVIDUALS

In the preceding chapters we identified some high-risk individuals whose actions and attitudes increase the risk of your relationship becoming sexualized. We hope that being aware of these dangerous individuals will help you to identify them and thereby reduce your risks.

The Sexual Manipulator

Be on the lookout for the sexual manipulator—the individual we outlined in chapters 5 and 6. These manipulators are difficult to recognize immediately. As soon as you ascertain their real motives, terminate the relationship.

Remember to be prepared for their denial. Manipulators are generally intelligent, cunning, and articulate. You will probably need to maintain your perspective of their behavior and actions in the face of denial or even hostility. Consistently state and defend your personal boundaries. Stand firm in your resolve to bring their sexual manipulation to light.

The Sexual Climber

If you are in a position of prominence or power, you will need to watch out for sexual climbers who see you as a way to advance their own personal position. Climbers will use whatever means necessary to seduce you. No matter what other enticements they initially offer, eventually they will attempt to introduce a sexual component into your relationship, hoping to use it as glue to bind you to them more tightly.

Spotting sexual climbers quickly can also be difficult. Be suspicious of anyone who seems to have your satisfaction or happiness as their only goal in life. Within marriage, that's paradise. Outside of marriage, it's puzzling. Maintain a healthy skepticism, especially if a disparity of position separates you. Watch, also, for the inevitable offer of sexual satisfaction. At that point, all doubt will be removed. Extricate yourself from the relationship without delay.

The Sexual Aggressor

Within a family, the risk comes from a sexual aggressor who usually abuses a younger sexual target. You may have recognized the pattern of the sexual aggressor outlined in chapter 7. Because of the age of the targets, this behavior is sheer aggression. If you are the adult victim of a sexual aggressor, you know the damage their aggression can cause.

If you are reading this book and are currently being victimized by a sexual aggressor, again, seek help immediately. Keep speaking out until someone comes to your defense.

One way to thwart sexual aggressors is for the adults within the immediate, extended, or blended family to monitor the different relationships within the family. If you have children, be attuned to their feelings about other family members. Provide a safe place for any child in your family to come to you for help.

ESCAPING SEXUAL IMMORALITY

God commands sexual purity. He created us with strong sexual desires, but he allows us to satisfy them only in marriage. Maintaining sexual integrity is not easy, but God never demands what we cannot do.

If You Are Unmarried

If you want to have sex, get married. Sex outside of marriage is immoral. God's Word is clear on this.

If you are engaging in a sexualized relationship outside of marriage, God does not condone what you are doing. He can forgive it, but you must cease immediately. If your partner does not agree, then you will have to withdraw from the relationship. If your partner does agree, the two of you should seriously consider your next step. It will be extremely difficult for you to stay "just friends" after a sexual component has been present in your relationship. The only realistic option is for the two of you to either split up or get married.

Of course, if you are single and inappropriately involved with someone who is married, you must withdraw from the relationship completely. Get another job, transfer to another city, do whatever it takes to burn the bridges between you and the immoral relationship. It could cost you your soul.

If You Are Married

The same advice is valid if you are married and having a sexual relationship with someone other than your spouse. Not only is your own soul in jeopardy, but also the soul of the person you profess to care about. Terminate the relationship now.

If you are married and have never slept with anyone but your mate, you may think congratulations are in order. However, before you pat yourself on the back, reflect on your relationships and the patterns you perpetuate within them. Take a minute to review the questions at the end of chapter 3. Be honest about the level of sexual integrity you maintain in all the other relationships in your life. Determine now to make the necessary adjustments to bring your actions and attitudes more in line with the sexual purity God has in mind for you.

Sexual Satisfaction

Throughout this book we have seen how strong sexual feelings can be. We have seen that some individuals will take advantage of this. If your marriage is not providing you a setting where you can experience sexual satisfaction, something may be wrong.

Some couples, because of health concerns, physical injury, or other considerations, cannot enjoy sexual satisfaction. This is a tragic situation and one that tests the bounds of marital commitment. If you are in a situation of this sort, you are not facing it alone. You have your spouse and your God with you. The other benefits to be shared in your marriage must compensate for and transcend your sexual desires. You are not permitted to seek sexual satisfaction outside of your marriage.

For some married people, sexual dysfunction is not physical, but mental, and may require extensive treatment and time to heal. Many competent Christian marriage counselors are well equipped to help you find a solution.

All couples go through dry periods when sexual interaction diminishes. This is normal, but this condition should not be prolonged. Paul gives us wise counsel in 1 Corinthians 7:5: "Do not deprive each other except by mutual consent and for a time, so that you may devote yourselves to prayer. Then come together again so that Satan will not tempt you because of your lack of self-control." God means for your marriage to be a continual source of sexual satisfaction.

Sometimes the marriage partners have simply fallen out of the habit of being sexual with each other. Some have not had sex for years. This is not a healthy marriage. This is not marriage as God intends it to be.

It is no coincidence that Paul's admonition to abstain only briefly from marital sex occurs directly after a long section on the dangers of sexual immorality. In fact, the stated reason for coming back together soon is so that Satan will not be able to tempt you into sin. One of your strongest defenses against sexual disasters is a strong, healthy sexual relationship within your marriage.

If the sexual part of your marriage is being spoiled by anger, bitterness, resentment, or embarrassment, seek help from a Christian marriage and family therapist or counselor. Work together with your therapist, and with God, to bring back the joys of sexual union within your marriage. God desires no less for you. Do not settle for less yourself.

——— Fuel for Thought ———

God did not arrange sex to leave you like a child in a candy store, unable to touch or taste. God knows you are a sexual being. He made you that way. God knows you will be tempted sexually. He made marriage to address that situation. God knows the society you live in. He expects you to influence it, not the other way around. God knows what is best for you sexually. His Word provides it.

God's Word provides the commandments we need to live with sexual integrity. Obey them.

"Here is the conclusion of the matter: Fear God and keep his commandments, for this is the whole duty of man. For God will bring every deed into judgment, including every hidden thing, whether it is good or evil" (Ecclesiastes 12:13–14).

MAY GOD'S SPIRIT ENABLE YOU *to discern high-risk situations and individuals. May he provide you insight to construct proper relationship boundaries and the strength of character to enforce them, even in the face of temptation. May God reveal his will to you as you seek integrity in all of your relationships. May God bless you always.*

Printed in the United States
By Bookmasters